ENDORSEMENTS FOR THE AUTHOR

Clare Erickson is an exceptional woman with an overflowing heart who blankets those around her with unconditional love and support. She is also one of the strongest Prayer Warriors I have ever known. While much of her strength comes from her background (which is conveyed in this life story), she has also used her social skills and abilities in Creative Arts to create small businesses and embark on enterprises that have touched everyone who has ever met her. This is the story of an admirable woman who makes a difference and leaves an imprint in her wake. I am proud to call her my friend.

Linda M. Olson, Maplewood, Minnesota

Clare never planned to become a Christian. She was running her own life and doing a lousy job. God used various circumstances to route Clare's life via Roman's Road as her pastor led her to Christ. She radiated love as she told girls of all ages about her joy in Christ at "Antie Clare's" Doll Hospital, Shop & Museum in North St. Paul, Minnesota. Through this medium, she touched the lives of all who entered her shop, as well as those who hear her speak in local churches and various meetings. Her life testimony bears witness to the power of Christ to change a life and give it a positive joy. I had the privilege of teaching her to say "PRAISE THE LORD!"

Loretta Jensen, wife of Pastor V. Richard Jensen

We all know there are times in life when a crisis happens and God sends someone to help us over the rough spots. Back in 1971 when Clare's stepson was attending Bible College and the team played a game in Iowa he received a very serious head injury. He was taken to Des Moines, Iowa where he remained in a coma and had four major surgeries and finally a titanium plate put in his head. He was there three months and had the renowned surgeon who would have gone to Pres. Kennedy had he lived a bit longer. This one event in life brought her closer to my family. I used to think when hardships came Clare's way; she just seemed to take them in her stride. I learned the secret of her strength during this ordeal. Clare wasn't alone; she was placing her trust in the Lord. She said I was a blessing, but now I see that she is a blessing to so many wherever God takes her. I believe you will find Clare's visit with you as you read her story will be very meaningful. She is a woman with many talents and gifts. She was a successful businesswoman, a much sought-after authority in the wonderful world of dolls. She was a devoted wife, loving mother, grandmother, cherished friend, became an International Doll Doctor, as well as most importantly, a committed Christian who lives for the Lord every day.

Dear friend, Jan Boleman-Rommereim

"Antie Clare," the "International Doll Doctor" for 35 years, loved to restore dolls and animals as well as entertain young girls at Victorian birthday tea parties. When she was young she was a mommie, a teacher, or a nurse and sold nectar by the side of their road. She became an X-ray technician for years and later began to collect and restore more dolls. (She never knew God needed doll doctors.) Clare is assertive, practical, intelligent, a workaholic, goal orientated, as well as a lot of fun and a "people person" because she cares about people's greatest needs. She is caring, loyal, and has a strong faith in God and became a dynamic speaker with dolls, history and her testimony. We first met in church over 28 years ago and became prayer partners that day. I rejoice to see her favorite verse come true: "Thou wilt show me Thy path of life. In Thy presence is fullness of joy, and at Thy right hand are pleasures forever more." Psalm 16:11

Lou Koehnle

Clare Erickson loves dolls and since 1970 has been collecting, restoring, and speaking on the wonderful world of dolls. She owned and operated "Antie Clare's" Doll Hospital, Shop & Museum in North St. Paul, Minnesota. The shop consisted of an admitting room with a doll crib where the children would tuck their doll or bear and it would be there when they were notified it was ready to go home. Dolls, figurines, lamps, statues, stuffed animals, and novelty items from all over the world were restored in the larger hospital, which could be viewed over a Dutch door. Big Bird from Children's Hospital was probably the most famous and frequent patient. Clare also had a magnificent website until she retired

She started many doll clubs and gave seminars, appraisal clinics, presentations for conventions, historical societies, clubs, retreats, mother-daughter functions, adult education classes, Christian Woman's groups and speeches all over Minnesota, Wisconsin, North and South Dakota, Iowa, Indiana, Florida, and Alaska. She has appeared on Good Company several times, PM Magazine, special features on KSTP and WCCO TV and programs on KSTP and KTIS radio. Articles appeared in *Doll Reader*, *Virtue* magazine, *Midwest Living*, *Dental News*, *Power for Living* and *Teddy Bear* periodicals, many newspapers and two doll books, *Dolls* and *Minnesota Christmas*. Clare is involved in her church and was a member of White Bear Avenue Business Association, Oakdale Business Association, and North St. Paul Business Association and also the Historical Societies, Board of Historic Design and Review, and a long time board member of Metro Woman's Center. "Antie Clare" has a dynamic life story that relates to young and old alike and shares her dolls and personal faith in Christ.

Good friend and special Doll Doctor, Sharon Checkalski

Clarice Erickson
Author & Speaker
Found, Forgiven Forever

1045 West Larpenteur Ave.
Roseville, MN 55113
651-487-2676

clarice.erickson@gmail.com

N,
R!

Faith

To Dani
love &
God Bless You
Clarice

by
CLARICE ERICKSON

xulon PRESS

FOUND, FORGIVEN, FOREVER!
My Journey of Faith
by Clarice Erickson

Printed in the United States of America

ISBN 9781629521794

Unless otherwise indicated, Bible quotations are taken from the King James Version of the Bible.

Book cover montage by David Welder

www.xulonpress.com

I dedicate this book to my family . . .

Paul, Rodney, Stephen, Sean, Rebecca, Douglas, and Greg—
you and all the grandchildren and great grands are my "gems."
I hold the good and precious memories of Marvin in my heart.

MY FAMILY

Ruth Hall & Harry Hop—born, 1910; married, 1933
(deceased—Dad, 1985; Mom, 1988)
Beverly—born, 1934
Winnie—born, 1935
Clarice—born, 1937
Bruce—born, 1939

Clarice & Jack Doyle (1956–1967)
Gregory & Monica Doyle
Douglas & Tessie Doyle
Sean Doyle

Clarice & Marvin Erickson (1968–1984)
Stephen & Jeanna Erickson
Rodney & Louise Erickson
Rebecca & John Mingo
Paul & Elizabeth Erickson

Grandchildren
Ryan, Zarah, Hillary, Ed, Ella, Heather, Waylon, Jodi,
John, Jon, Bjorn, Jessie, Lief, Mandy, Sam & Ian

Great Grandchildren
Cyrena, Malachi, Jocelyn, Anya, Lillia, Isabella,
Dynamite & Askel

CONTENTS

INTRODUCTION

$\mathcal{M}$y life started during the time of the Great Depression. I have a wonderful, interesting, and historic genealogy and was raised in a loving home where everything seemed perfect. My family helped me discover my talents. While not worthy of Oscar awards, they show genuine love and service to others.

I had many ideas and talents to experience and a strong urge to include others and multiply their joy and friendship with mine. For this I had no maps or directions for God's plan for me. I did know I needed something more satisfying so I looked for this in activities, family, and friends to no avail.

What I lacked was that deep inner peace and comfort. So, I questioned my worth and where I could find both peace and comfort. But God did know me! He knew where I was all of the time AND, of course, He had plans for my life. He used my love of people and even dolls to keep wooing me to Him.

I am sharing with you many of my life experiences. You may be surprised by my strength and focus on fulfillment. I have touched many lives! Yes, I am bold and assertive while being friendly.

God never gives up on people, so you will see His presence and direction many times in my life story. And, now I can say, "I FOUND it, He FORGAVE me, and FOREVER I will live with my Savior!"

Chapter 1

MY BEGINNING YEARS OF LIFE

*O*nce upon a time . . . or what would have been printed in my baby book had it not burned up in our house fire.

(The following message was written later by my mom, Ruth.)

Clarice Mae was born at the new Baldwin Hospital on July 17, 1937, a late Saturday afternoon. It was a beautiful day but hot and the girls and I (Ruth) *took lunch to Dad who was cultivating corn with the horses on the Bernscott place. We toured the big, vacant house and then went home and took naps.*

Cousin Dotty was living with us and when she saw me putting on the new hoover apron (big front with large pockets across the bottom, overlapped, and tied in back), *she knew it was time.* (Mom loved her hoover apron on hot days, being able to wear fewer articles of clothing.) *She was right. Clarice was born about 10 p.m. and weighed about 8 pounds. She was a darling little blonde. Gramma Hall* (Alma, Grampa Hall's second wife) *never had a baby to name, so since they paid the hospital bill of $37, we could have the* *baby in a hospital; she wanted the baby to be "Clarice." The middle name, Mae, was after her niece in Minneapolis.*

Clarice used to wiggle around on the floor sitting in a metal pie tin and walked at about a year. She had pneumonia her first winter and so did the Vanden Berg's boy so I listened on the phone to hear what Doc Olson said to do for him and I did it for her. (Older sister Winnie had it the next winter.)

Clarice grew well and was the little sister to Beverly and Winifred. The older girls were fighting again and Clarice came to the basement stairs calling, "Mommie, come, dem kids fightin' again." When she was 2 1/2 and little brother, Bruce (Butch) *spilled his food on the highchair, she said, "Ain't you shamed yourself?"*

She liked school and always had big ideas and was involved in many things. She had many friends and people liked her.

P.S. On her first Christmas, she was the baby Jesus in the manger for the nativity scene and did not cry at all.

My mom, Ruth Hall, was a schoolteacher when she met my dad, Harry Hop. He drove a milk truck in the neighborhood where she roomed and passed by the Three Willow School where she taught. It wasn't long before her students were aware of their courting and would watch for him to drive by the building, which caused quite a commotion. When my folks were married in 1933, they moved east of Hammond, Wisconsin to live on a farm. They soon bought a small farm northeast of Baldwin. My oldest sister, Beverly, was born in 1934; followed by another sister, Winifred

(Winnie), in 1935, before I was born in 1937. Our little brother, Bruce (Butch), was born two years later. My sisters and I just loved him! It was easy for us to spoil Bruce!

On one very hot Monday morning in August our life on the farm changed very quickly! My six-year-old sister, Beverly, was staying with our grandparents south of Hammond. Winnie, Butch, and I were sleeping quite soundly upstairs. Our fourteen-year-old cousin, Dottie, was also asleep upstairs. Only three years old, I don't remember that day, but other family members have shared memories about it many times.

That morning, as usual, Dad went to put the cows in the barn and got ready to milk them. For some reason, Mom pondered about whether to help with the milking or start preparing the noon meal. She finally walked back to the summer kitchen and started the oil stove, after which she joined Dad in the barn. They usually finished the milking before leaving the building; however, Mom was feeling a strong need to go to the milk house and check the water level of the stock tank. When she reached the barn door, her hands and feet "froze" and she let out a blood-curdling scream, "the back kitchen is on FIRE!"

Dad and Mom ran to the house. Dad dashed for the phone and called their party line for help, thinking that most neighbors would be doing chores and might have seen the smoke from their farms. Trying to be calm, Mom screamed for her niece to wake up and help carry the children downstairs and outside. In our pajamas, Dotty took Butch and me to the nearest neighbor's house. She let Winnie stay in the neighbor's ditch to watch the fire. (Winnie, who was five years old at the time, remembers seeing the whole house collapsing in flames.)

The fire raged and spread. Mom had to decide quickly if she should carry out some food while pleading with Dad to retrieve her wedding rings from the finial of her dresser upstairs. As Dad ran up the stairs to the second floor bedrooms, he heard the steps collapse behind him leaving no way to return. By that time, a few neighbors had gathered on our front lawn. Dad grabbed the rings and used his left arm to break the window, causing a long jagged gash and severing a vein. He jumped to the ground and rolled with blood flying.

There was no medical help available, so Mom quickly removed her pink, baggy bloomers; tore them into wide strips; and wrapped the cloth as tightly as possible around his arm. It worked to stop the bleeding!

Before long, Doc Olson arrived and did a great job cleaning and stitching my dad's wound. He was very surprised that Mom had applied enough pressure with the "big pink bandage" to stop the blood from gushing from the vein. Dad's left arm healed well, but we could always see the long scar.

The house was completely burned in half an hour, but all six of us survived! What a wonderful miracle! Through it all, my folks counted the blessings and miracles, appreciated the help of friends and relatives, and gave thanks for how great God really was to them! He sure knew where we were!

To replace the house that burnt, Dad and Mom designed and built a new two-story house on a full basement with over two-thirds of the help coming from community members. My folks spoke often about how wonderful people are and how you don't really know that until tragedy hits.

Relatives and neighbors "talked" about the construction because Dad actually built a bathroom "inside of our new house." No one else in the neighborhood had one of those. Supposedly they didn't need an inside facility, but we sure loved it! We also appreciated Dad's special way to have bathroom privacy. He built a set of drawers in the wall that could be pulled out next to the door to hold it closed.

The new basement was also a special place for my sisters, brother, and me to play. It was fun to run around on the cement floor and even roller skate on it as we got older.

Another special feature in our new house was the breakfast nook in the kitchen. The bench seats could be lifted up making it possible to store things there like Christmas gifts and fruitcakes, which Mom was famous for. I don't remember seeing another nook like this until we moved to Hammond, Wisconsin in 1945. In that house Dad built another set of bench seats that had heated vents underneath it. Years later, when Mom got back to the fruitcake stored in the bench seats for one of our weddings, it was pretty bad, having been warmed for weeks! (Too late!)

I also fondly remember the times when Dad poured cement at the entrance of an outbuilding on the farm. We made our handprints and footprints in the wet cement. That was a "big deal" for us because it meant we had "arrived" in our imagination. We almost always had a sandbox near the house, which was so much fun to play in. Our chickens and cats liked it, too!

One of our neighbors, the Sather family, had four girls who we loved to play with. We would mail notes to each other via our "post office"—some cans in the rock pile located halfway between our houses. One time when I was about six years old, the families who belonged to Mom's True Blue 4-H Club held a meeting at the Sather's house.

While the adults discussed some issues, we kids headed to the haymow (the upper story of a barn). Oh, what great fun we thought we would have! A huge mound of hay had already been unloaded and a wagon full of hay was sitting in the middle of the haymow next to the mound. The big kids were jumping from the mound of hay onto the wagon loaded with hay, a short distance away. Soon, it was my turn to be a "big girl"! I was sitting fearfully on the mound of hay rather than standing, ready to jump. This was not fun at all! One of the big kids pushed me, causing me to slide off between the haymow and hay wagon. I cracked my head on the wagon's iron wheel and landed very near the hay shoot—an opening in the floor—for feeding the cows below! Someone ran to get my mom. My injury to the skull bled profusely. Mom was handed a huge handful of Irmegarde's handkerchiefs and used them to press firmly on my head as we raced to the clinic.

My experiences in a hospital or other medical rooms were always scary. I was afraid that all of the instruments would be used on me and the smell was next to dying. The doctor stitched after shaving off a circle of hair from my head. Thinking back, I count it also a miracle. I should not have been playing in the haymow at all!

While living on the farm, we had a Collie dog, named Pal, and a pony. My family also had an unusual "zoo" of animals. Pal helped us care for the sheep, cats, chickens, a goat, cows, pigs, and horses.

I also remember the time when Bev and I were wearing boots and "mucking" in the wet and muddy garden by walking and pulling our boots out of the mud with our feet, or "sucking them up." We considered this a new game and a funny noisy one, too! Dad saw us and yelled to get out! We couldn't resist doing a few more "mucks," so we didn't move fast enough out of the garden. He came and had us meet him at the bottom of the basement steps for a spanking. Of course, our stockings and the inside of our boots were a muddy mess and he was not happy with us. Dad did not spank hard and we started giggling. This brought Mom down there to spank us. She really did spank hard, which did hurt, and we cried and didn't muck in the mud again. (I considered this a small miracle!)

Ruth Hall and Harry W. Hop, married on June 1, 1933

Bruce, Harry (their dad), Beverly, Clarice, Ruth
(their mom), and Winnie in their home

House built after the fire

Hopyard
Country School

Chapter 2

OUR HOME IN HAMMOND

*D*aily life changed for my family when we moved off the farm and into Hammond, Wisconsin—a small town at that time. I was nine years old and a student in third grade. While we lived in the farmhouse, my dad had several major surgeries and contracted undulant fever (from raw or unpasteurized milk) when he went to Montana to hunt, so it was best for him to leave the farming and milking.

In Hammond, it seemed like you knew most of the people who lived there. My folks were acquainted with the parents of our friends, which didn't happen in a larger city. While Dad delivered oil to farmers, Mom was busy with the household since our grandparents lived with us. She also enjoyed being involved with the local 4-H Club, Homemakers, local plays at the Community Hall, two very large gardens, coffee clutches, substitute teaching, the parent-teacher association, and church work. Mom excelled as a great leader and speaker, whereas my dad preferred being in the background and enjoyed the challenge of building or repairing almost anything.

Mom also played the piano and sang. Many times when we were all together at home on a Sunday afternoon, she would play through the hymnals. These were special times, hearing the hymns about the love and security of God. The music made me feel good.

We all sang in school choirs and other groups. This interest in music for my folks and siblings has continued through the years. As an adult, Bruce sang karaoke with his friend Carole.

I helped care for the gardens and strawberry and raspberry patches and often felt the work was too hard, which called for a "pity party" on my part, but that didn't make it any easier. So, one afternoon for fun, my friend and I put our initials on our backs with surgical tape before beginning to pull weeds. You can imagine what happened! I experienced many sunburns until I matured and learned to protect my skin from the sunshine.

While growing up, I also never figured out how we could have a "charge it to my dad" bill at Larson's grocery store! I thought this store was more intriguing than any other place in town because of the notions section. So, one time while browsing, I stole a small box of paper clips. This was not wise because Mom saw what I had taken and marched me up the block back to the store where I had to apologize to Mr. Larson for my deed. (I think of that lesson every time I use a paper clip. It certainly kept me from stealing ever again.) As a ten-year-old child, I didn't need paper clips anyway, but today, I'm so glad for the forgiveness of my mom and Mr. Larson.

While living in Hammond, my best friends were Kay, Kathy and Karin—all close neighbors. We played in our attic when it wasn't too hot or too cold, or outside by the lilac bushes with orange crates for makeshift rooms in nice weather. We played dress-up, school, house, store, and church. My friends and I would rearrange the attic for whatever our imaginative play idea was for that day. I was the "dolly girl" in the family and dolls were my babies. This meant I had to have a pretend husband, so I said my "boyfriend," whomever I liked at the time, was the daddy to my dolls and he was in Korea. Of course, if I told my friends or family, they teased me about it. Pat was a favorite "husband" and he never knew it until we were adults and both married with families. (Winnie still teases me about the boys "I was in love with," especially at our high school reunions!)

I especially remember playing at Karin's house on one special summer day. Karin had a great baby-size doll with short curly hair. The arms had broken away from the shoulders and she set it down to lean on the garbage can and threw the beautiful coat and cap on it that her grandmother, "Mor-Mor," made for her dolls. I took the doll to my home because Karin didn't want it. Mom repaired it and marched me back to Karin's mom to return it. They said I could keep the doll—she became my very favorite one! I discovered years later that the doll was an Effanbee with hair made from caracul (lamb's wool). When I was much older and working in the doll repair and museum business, that special doll went with me to all of my speeches. I still have her to this day!

Also on beautiful summer days, Karin and I loved to lie on the slope in my backyard and look for shapes in the cloud formations. She liked my mom's dill pickles, so I would bring out a quart of them and that was our snack for the cloud show. This was my idea of heaven!

As we grew up, my folks encouraged my siblings and me to be at our house with friends. What wonderful memories I have! When the country kids were snowbound, some of them would sleep over. We would often host a sock hop, filling the living room with friends and lively music. The same was true after the basketball games when friends would gather there. If other parents couldn't find their children, they called the Hop's household and learned "Yes, they are here, too." (My siblings and I were discouraged from going to a local restaurant because we didn't have the extra money and we were not allowed to be out too late.) Almost every Saturday morning, Mom had bread dough rising and baking. Those who had stayed the night would wake up to the wonderful aroma of freshly baked bread and looked forward to eating her delicious baked goods. My favorite of all was her cinnamon rolls, which were gone by the end of the day! (Great memory, Mom!)

During my teenage years, I was tall with a sturdy build; however, I couldn't run fast or catch a ball, so I was usually the last one chosen for a team. BUT, I still cared about people and felt sorry for the ones who were teased, left out, or called names. It hurt me to watch others being picked on. In junior high, I could be a cheerleader and, of course, I couldn't do handstands or cartwheels but the squad could have built a pyramid on me!

School was always a wonderful experience for me. Mom was actually my teacher for a while at the country school (Hopyard) that we attended and a great encourager through my school years. Later, one of Mom's best friends was my speech and English teacher. She was tough, expecting a lot from her students, and the best teacher I ever had. Many other students felt that way, too. Mrs. Hartwig also directed the class plays! In one of the plays I portrayed a "dud" of a maid who was in love with a "husky man from Sandusky." No glamour in that role! I had to wear my hair rolled up in curlers and covered with a scarf in the shape of a triangle, which was wrapped around my head with the ends tied together in a knot on top and tucked into the folds.

Driver's Education was much different in the 1950s, than today. Mom was a great teacher. She had us drive four miles to the neighboring town and back on the country gravel roads with her. The first time I drove at night was when we came back from southeast Wisconsin after attending a family reunion on Mom's side. I drove for several hours and hardly slept at all after we arrived at home. Every time I closed my eyes I visualized headlights coming at me. Fourteen years later with seven children growing up in our home, as a parent, I was so glad to have experienced that. I felt my children and other students also needed driver's training experiences on city streets, freeways, and on roads at night. Over the years, I trained twelve people to drive my car!

On Labor Day in 1954, just prior to starting my senior year of high school, our church family held a picnic at the pool park in River Falls, Wisconsin. We were enjoying swimming in the water. I had just dived off the high board and was resurfacing. One of the guys jumped off the board like a canon ball and landed on the top of my head and face, pushing me under the water's surface. Instinctively, I raised my hands to my face and saw lots of blood. I thought I was finished—dead! Having passed out in the water, I regained consciousness in the girl's side of the bathhouse and learned that my face was a mess. Off to the doctor for stitches on my lips and mouth! My nose was broken and my eyes hurt! They began to turn purple and red. It didn't take long for my face to be black and blue with a very swollen nose, eyes, and lips. This was not the glamorous look I had planned for starting my last year in high school! My glasses wouldn't fit and, of course, everyone saw the bruises and had to ask, "What happened?" (I could have drowned! Once again, God gave me another miracle!)

As a teenager, I hadn't really learned how to communicate with God. So, when life was great I felt happy, but when it wasn't, I begged Him to help me.

Clarice holding her favorite doll
named "Sweetie Pie" (Effanbee
doll), given to her by Karin

Chapter 3

THOSE BEAUTIFUL
BROWN EYES

During my junior year of high school, I encountered a young man—tall and handsome with dark hair and amazing brown eyes. His name was Jack and I met him at a dance that I wasn't supposed to attend. He was four years older than me and was enlisted in the Army. I was thrilled to be able to sing the song, "Beautiful Brown Eyes." Have you ever heard of "singing a certain song" being on your hopeful to-do list?

I started to date Jack, writing letters to him while he was in the service and continued to date him during the two summers he worked in Alaska and when he attended classes at the University of River Falls, Wisconsin.

Jack was raised in El Paso, Wisconsin on the Rush River. His parents were divorced. His mom needed to work at a "big" job. She advertised in a local paper for a couple to care for her two sons. Herman and Alice responded to her call for help. They didn't have children of their own. Jack and his brother were the first of around thirty children that they helped raise. Jack grew up in their home before moving to St. Paul after high school graduation to work and then served three years in the Army. My first introduction to Herman and Alice was very special to me. They knew Jack as a little boy and they fell in love with me so much that the first time I met them I had to have two pieces of apple pie—each with a piece of cheese on the side.

Whenever I visited them, I enjoyed helping in the house with Alice, shampooing and styling her hair, tidying up the kitchen, and whatever else that needed to be done. Every weekend Herman and Alice prepared for an onslaught of people coming down to their park on the Rush River, so their huge yard had to be mowed the hard way with a hand mower.

As a result I connected with other people who were at Herman and Alice's house. One person for sure was Merlin (a young lad who lived with Herman and Alice as Jack was easing out his stay). He was like a younger brother to me, and later his wife, Denise, became a special dear friend.

In the spring of 1955, I graduated from high school and planned to attend the University of Wisconsin to study occupational therapy. On the day before the graduation ceremony, I was free so I bussed to downtown St. Paul to apply for a summer job. No one would hire me because when asked about my future plans, I answered, "Yes, I plan to go to University in the fall." Later that afternoon I rode the bus to Minneapolis hoping to see my sister's friend in the lab at Swedish Hospital. While standing and waiting by the elevator door in the hospital, Carrie came out, coincidentally, on her way to having coffee in another building. (I soon learned to drink coffee!) Carrie and her friends were working in the X-ray department instead of the laboratory so they took me back to meet the staff and see the facility. After the tour, I decided to sign up for classes, which started at the University of Minnesota on the following Monday. I had to hustle back home, get some references and talk to my folks STAT (my new word in that field)! I was quite excited about my new goal and I have never been sorry this happened. God opened a door in my life that was best for me. This decision also meant that I needed to rent a room in a house in Minneapolis to be able to work in the hospital while attending classes.

During the fifteen months following my high school graduation, I attended classes at the University of Minnesota and completed the Swedish Hospital training to become an X-ray technician. My folks were glad to have me around a bit more. My dad paid $500 for this training. They were so proud of me!

At first, I lived in a turret on the third floor of an old house with a classmate. Later, I moved in with four senior X-ray students who offered me a chance to rent with them on the whole upper floor of an older, big, two-story, brick house on Chicago Avenue in Minneapolis. We walked the twelve blocks to the Swedish Hospital on nice days, wearing all white uniform dresses, nylons, and shoes. This made me think of how proud I was to be involved in hospital work.

During my studies, I also learned "It's always too late to say I'm sorry." This was drummed into me many times at work. I still easily recall one of the worst mistakes I made and wonder if Dr. Idstrom ever told his colleagues his version of the story. At the time, I was assisting Dr. Idstrom and my job was to prepare the room for a spinogram on a patient. One of two basins was to be used for disinfecting Dr. Idstrom's hands before his rubber gloves went on and the other one contained the merthiolate for use on the patient's back. The liquids smelled similar to me; in the dark I held the merthiolate basin for him to dip both hands into and then into the gloves. When the test was finished, I took his used gloves and saw his bright orange-red hands and the face of a very angry doctor. My first big miracle in the department was I did graduate! Perhaps Dr. Idstrom used my mistake as a teaching lesson over the years.

Melva became a close dear friend because we were both new residents in the big house and soon we became engaged to our boyfriends. We often cooked and shared meals together. The other three gals ate our leftovers because they were going out on dates a lot and we were not. Melva and I also became acquainted with "call" work, especially during weekends and at night so we could actually get paid. At midnight in the cafeteria, huge trays of peanut butter and bacon sandwiches were offered free to the staff on call. We learned to like those immediately and I still do!

During training, one thing that I was not taught was how to hold a basin in the right position so a sick patient on a gurney could upchuck into the basin, instead of on me, or all down the front of me. Those little kidney-shaped basins were not large enough; sometimes I really got it, even in my shoes.

I remember one lovely lady who came in for radiation treatments. Her left breast had decayed and was filled with maggots. This experience was something I will never forget. We became good friends since she ended up staying on the floor where I worked, which made it easier for me to see her during my break times. She was a Christian Scientist. Jack's mother was also a Christian Scientist and she often told me about her beliefs. I grew up attending church but did not know Jesus personally as my Savior. Jack held no special religious beliefs and kept it that way through life. We needed the miracle of salvation but I didn't know it at the time.

This lovely woman had not married and seemed pleased to have me check in on her once or twice a day and also see her at the time of her radiation. I massaged her body a lot and sometimes just visited. Oh, how I wish that I could have introduced her to Christ and eternal life back in 1956. This memory causes me to be bold for the Lord today.

During that time, Jack attended River Falls College and completed fishery surveys all over Minnesota and Wisconsin. The following summer he traveled to Alaska to count fish (mostly salmon) migrating up the streams to spawn. We planned to be married on Sept. 15, 1956, after which he would continue his education at the University of Washington in Seattle.

It was a busy summer in 1956 with Jack working in Alaska. I finished my training, earning the degree of X-ray Technologist, and was registered. What a proud day that was for me being "pinned" during the graduation ceremony and having my folks supporting my accomplishment!

Three days before the wedding Jack returned from Alaska, sporting a big bushy beard. We both gave blood in town because I was working at the Blood Drive and as soon as we were done we took off to buy a new car in Baldwin and a new trailer house in Knapp. This trailer appeared to be huge, reminding me of the movie, "Long, Long Trailer" with Lucille Ball. Our trailer was 28 feet long and 8 feet wide. Dad helped Jack remove the front bunk room because we didn't plan to have children while living there. We had the trailer moved to my folks' backyard where it was convenient to store the shower gifts and let friends and relatives go in and check it out.

Jack's mom gave us a nice rehearsal dinner in Hudson. Before the rehearsal, Jack had shaved his beard and I didn't even notice the change! My family and friends gave me a hard time and I just thought, oh well, we should have been kissing more and I might have noticed!

Friday evening after the rehearsal dinner, Jack and I took friends into the trailer to show them the interior and our wedding gifts. When leaving, we accidentally locked both of the door keys inside on the table—each thinking the other one had a key. Ohhhh man, that was a late night in the rain! Vern helped Jack to take the jolicy door window out, which had zillions of screws to remove and then replace.

I heard two carloads of my X-ray technician friends were coming from Minneapolis and I wanted our china, crystal and silverware samples to display! The next morning, my wonderful "Uncle Lloyd" drove me to St. Paul to buy a place setting to show off. (Today, I am sure no one cares or can even remember what the place setting was. I am still a strong-willed gal.) No doubt, I really must have tested my folks on getting back on time for my wedding. My hair never did get re-curled for the ceremony!

That forenoon before our 4 p.m. wedding, Jack shaved his mustache. When I saw him next, he looked like the handsome guy I knew! Oh, NO, another crisis back at the house—Carol wasn't able to find the rings in the side pocket of my suitcase. So Jack and I were married using my father's ring and Mary Monson's ring. The prelude was exceptionally long as we waited for the rings to arrive!

The rest of September 15th went well. Mom had decorated the church windows with candles and since the weather was very hot during that late afternoon, the guests sitting near them had to open the windows. Many ladies helped with the food for the reception and provided flowers from their gardens. Mom kept a list of all of them. I loved all of these friends and appreciated the hometown advantages. I love to look at the photographs and see the family and friends and memories that go with them. I had no idea where we were honeymooning until after the wedding. Jack and I spent two days in the Lake Pepin area with very windy, rainy weather, so unfortunately we didn't get out on the water. However, we did get out to eat!

On Monday after a short honeymoon, we returned to my folks' place. Earlier in the day, Dad had pulled the trailer up the slope in the backyard. It was hooked up to our vehicle and then Jack and I were hugging good-byes with everyone.

Heading west, towing the trailer behind us, Jack and I left the state of Wisconsin. The new Hudson bridge was finished and open, so we drove across it. I remember turning to gaze in the direction of my childhood home and wondering when I'd ever come back. That was a brief lonesome attack!

After a quiet and somber ride, Jack started to tease me about the mountains, saying how low and small they were. (Later, I found them to be so majestic. I was thrilled every time I saw them!) As we traveled west, it was like an open door to my new life as Jack's wife and the grandeur of God's beautiful creation.

Jack and Clarice bought this Dodge car and "long" mobile home and drove it to Seattle. This was their home for five years.

John (Jack) Doyle
as a young man

Jack's dad (Thomas Doyle) with cousin Robin,
years later

Clarice Hop and John (Jack) P. Doyle, married on
Sept. 15, 1956

Happy wedding day
for Jack and Clarice

Jack's mom (Winnie)
with Clarice and Jack

Chapter 4

WESTWARD HO!

*W*hile pressing on, Jack and I took turns driving to arrive sooner—making only one overnight stop—pulling the "long" trailer behind our car. That decision was not wise! Jack needed to start at the University and I had a job lined up in the X-ray department at Swedish Hospital in downtown Seattle.

I was at the wheel when it was time to make our only overnight stop. Jack got out to direct me through a sharp left turn and up a nice long hill because he had planned for us to stay at this campground. I scraped the driver's side of our new trailer on a wooden guide pole. (It was in my way, of course!) I started to cry and wanted to get out of the vehicle, but the ditch was too steep for me to step out. Jack let me know what was on his mind and then told me how to rectify the turn by slowly backing up the car and trailer and trying it again. Driving over the mountains was a piece of cake for me after that experience!

Arriving in Seattle, we settled in Trailer City (off Interstate Highway 99 north of Seattle) for Jack's first year of school. We met a couple from Woodville and spent fun "cheap" times together. Our new friend, Marion, was pregnant and I had just found out we were also expecting a child. My pregnancy was a big miracle from God. Jack didn't want to have children and had great plans to ship me off to Japan for an abortion.

I had to be extremely careful when working in the X-ray department because I wanted to wait as long as possible to tell them so that I could keep my job. My baby was due June 9th. On my last day at work, the crew was "loose" in the afternoon and decided to take X rays of the baby to see what sex it was. It didn't show that information but I was able to take the films.

I planned to spend the summer with my folks. With my doctor's permission to fly in my ninth month, I departed to Minneapolis (nearest airport to my folk's house in Wisconsin). No one asked me for my permission slip from the doctor and I didn't say anything about it because labor pains had not started.

During the first week back in the Midwest, I had the flu and wondered if I could actually upchuck a baby. When that quieted down, Dad brought home a bottle of castor oil and explained that his mother would have taken this to start the delivery. Oh my land, I made an even closer relationship with Mom's bathroom!

Our first son was born on the 28th of June, nearly three weeks late, and that was not the first time he made his parents wait. I was in labor all day and was admitted into the small community hospital where I had been born. Finally, during the dinner hour when the staff was busy and the doctor had gone home for supper, my mom knitted and watched as I tried to be quiet and undemanding and also trying not to push too hard. When the labor pains became more intense, her knitting speed matched my need! It wasn't long before she quietly went out (no, actually ran!) to find a nurse who immediately flew around to help this baby boy come into the world. My work was done! Before the nurse cleaned up the baby's mouth and checked his breathing, someone had reached the doctor at home. He walked in to take charge as the whole hospital knew what had happened in the labor room. The doctor arrived just in time to stitch up a tear and take care of the baby. What a relief and after that everything was all okay! Jack and I had a precious newborn son with dark brown eyes.

Our baby boy was named Gregory Bradford. There were only two other babies in the nursery, both boys, and both named Gregory! I kept our son's given name because my baby Gregory would not be living in that area forever.

Baby Gregory and I spent a wonderful summer in 1957 with my folks. About the time Jack returned to Seattle after completing his summer research project, my mom and a wonderful friend, Jean, who was my bridesmaid and lived with my folks, drove Greg and me back to Seattle. We camped along the route and Mom got excited about washing out some cloth diapers in a beautiful stream in Glacier Park. (Of course, Greg doesn't remember tenting, cooking, and seeing the great scenic wonders.) God answered my prayers for a family! It was hard for me to return to work knowing that this little miracle from God would be loved and nurtured by a baby-sitter.

While working in the X-ray department at Swedish Hospital, I would save used clear film to make bookmarks shaped as the cross. On those pieces, I sketched flowers and the question "What Is God Like?" Yes, I was searching just like so many others, wondering, "Am I good enough?"

Two years later after settling in Trailer City, Jack and I had to move our trailer out because Interstate 99 was to be widened. The trailer court property had been taken for the improvement project. As fast as we could, we secured a new place closer to the campus, which made it possible for Jack to bike to school in good weather. The corner lot that we leased hadn't been used for anything but growing weeds. It was even a bit larger than the adjacent lots in the row. The trailers were so close together we could see into our neighbor's dining area, just like they could look into ours. I was very pregnant with our second child, much to Jack's dismay. Of course, it was definitely his child, too!

One day our propane cooking stove was repaired. We were unaware that the repairman had not secured the coupling for the gas line in the back of the stove before leaving. Jack was reading when I got home that evening and I plunked Greg into his high chair with something to fascinate him. I washed up and started to prepare our supper. With a lit match, I tried to start the stove, but all four burners wouldn't light. Jack was disgusted, so he came over to do it. By that time a lot of gas had come up behind the stove.

When Jack lit a match, it exploded into a kitchen fire. As I stood closest to the outside door, Jack commanded me to turn the gas off out front—"NOW!" In my haste to run down the three steps, I fell—being too top heavy to stay upright—onto my abdomen and arm, hoping to break my arm instead of injuring our baby. I couldn't catch my breath. Our neighbors Robert and Carol were eating their dinner and thinking that we were having a big fight, rushed to help me. Robert reached me first and I gasped, "Turn off the gas! Hurry! We have a big fire in the kitchen."

Bob turned the propane off out front and helped Jack put the kitchen fire out. I asked Carol to help me use the back door to get inside, help me onto my bed, and look at what was happening between my legs. I could feel the swelling that made it very hard to walk. I was crying just thinking about losing our baby, after which they assisted me into the car. Jack drove me to the emergency room at Swedish Hospital. It was a miracle that the trailer didn't explode or burn to the ground!

Bob and Carol took care of Greg (Carol became a great friend) while I stayed in the hospital because it was important that I didn't go into premature labor. Jack also missed a bit of school. After I was released, I did deskwork at the hospital and the staff was so good to me. (Our possibility of winning a lawsuit seemed certain. Yet the proceedings dragged on for three years. When the suit was finally resolved, Jack had graduated from the program and we were living in Canada.)

Douglas Patrick Doyle was born on July 30, 1959 with easy birthing. My doctor was so special and kind. He showed me how Doug's feet turned in like clubfeet and explained that if I held them for a "count" each time I changed his diapers, this therapy would straighten his little feet. It did!

We had to pay for the repairs to the kitchen after the fire and lost any payment from the wrongful repairs, but we were relieved to have it turn out as another great miracle. (God is so good!) This was one of those times when it seemed like life wasn't fair, yet it goes on.

My photo of Doug as a newborn shows his little feet turned in. When he was about five-years old, I caught him with a pair of little plastic scissors cutting around the bottom of the photo just up to his feet. I didn't kill the kid and he didn't use the cute little scissors for a while. That was 1964. If I were to bring up this story to Doug now, he would just give me the sweetest smile. He has dark brown eyes like his dad.

New baby boy Doug was born on
July 30, 1959.
His feet turned out perfect!
Wonderful miracle!

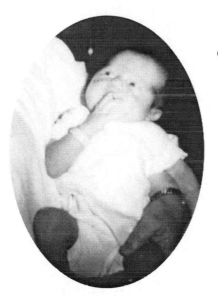

Gregory "thanking" the nurse
(born June 28, 1957)

Herman and Alice Jones (Jack's foster parents) with baby Greg

Chapter 5

ON THE ROAD AGAIN

*W*ithin a four-year span, we moved seven times and finally landed in a vacant one level row house in Union Circle near the University of Washington campus! Thank, God, each house had a large number because the units all looked alike. Our housing was quite international with interesting features; our collection of eclectic furniture fit in well. Greg had started school and was doing well. However, he did have trouble with Peter who played in our courtyard. Peter chased Greg with a big stick one too many times. I got a stick for Greg and encouraged him to go after Peter and let him have it. I followed to make certain we wouldn't be arrested and it worked! (Sort of a miracle for Greg!) Peter never chased him again.

While Jack was finishing another degree, I started a relief technician job and let the hospitals and bigger clinics know that I was available for vacation or emergency work. A gal in our court enjoyed watching the boys and the temporary work really caught on. This arrangement was great for us because I could say "No" if I couldn't fit it in my schedule.

It was a new experience for me to work in all the different departments. I loved what I did! I found I was quite skilled in working with the X-ray machines and film development in the dark rooms and watched carefully where others processed, laid, labeled, and filed films. When I wasn't busy, I would dust and polish the equipment. My service was noticed because no one else felt they were paid to do that.

The 1962 Seattle World's Fair or "Century 21 Exposition" was also going on while I handled relief X-ray work. I told my folks that if any friends came to Seattle, they could stay with us and/ or I would take them to the World's Fair and pick them up at an entrance. We had twenty different "stays" and/or "drop offs." Many people accepted my offer to be a guide and I learned quickly what time to stand in line for the happenings they would enjoy. I collected brochures to give the visitors before they toured the exhibits. Everything had lines, but timing could be more kind! Jack and the boys never got there but saw the tall Space Needle and the monorail often.

We lived in Union Circle for two years. Jack spent summers in Alaska conducting more research for his final degree. During the first summer, the boys and I stayed in the court; however, during the second summer I was pregnant, so I traveled back to New Richmond, Wisconsin with the two boys. That fall, Greg attended second grade where Mom taught. What a wonderful way that was to spend time with my folks and family and Jack's mother. Bonding was the best!

Our third baby was due early in December. Much to my surprise, it was near the due date and the baby wasn't coming. My doctor suggested that he should induce labor so that we could be ready to travel back to Alaska with Jack. It didn't work! For two weeks I had a horrible case of the flu. Gramma Ruth and I thought this child would come by mouth. It wasn't funny at the time and something we didn't count on.

As I was cleaning at my folks' house waiting to go into labor, the news came on the TV that President Kennedy had been shot. I was so sad and upset to think that someone took the life of our leader and our nation witnessed it all on television.

About a month later on Sunday, December 22, 1963, I didn't dare worship in church that morning with my family because the labor pains I felt were becoming very intense. Someone else was put in charge of meeting Jack at the Minneapolis Airport as I worked hard to bring this baby into the world. Jack and the stork were in a dead heat to arrive! Well, babies come when God plans for them and Jack was due to fly into the Twin Cities about 4 p.m.

Earlier that afternoon, my dad took Greg and Doug out to ice fish so they wouldn't hear me in labor and Mom cautiously watched the timing of my pains. I thought I was really helping by wrapping the family Christmas presents.

By the time we arrived at the hospital, the baby was ready to come out and join us! What a sweetie! At 4:15 p.m. Dr. Drury delivered son number three, Sean Thomas Doyle. Sean (Gaelic for *John*) was born in good health, shortly before his dad arrived. Sean also has dark brown eyes like his daddy!

Jack had a bad cold when he arrived. To ward it off, I was given a penicillin shot, which caused a severe reaction. This meant my bottom was fiery red! I stayed in the hospital for about five days while recovering (a very nice miracle!) from this terrible reaction to penicillin.

The folks gave me a new bathrobe, which I wore when I was permitted to go to their house for two hours on Christmas Eve. The hospital staff assured me they would take good care of Sean while I was gone. That evening at my folks' house, I opened gifts and ate good food while everyone asked about the baby and watched over me. The O'Connells gave Sean a Santa romper. Even though it was a bit big, I dressed him in the romper when we were released from the hospital to go to my folks' house.

After Christmas, Jack and the two older boys took off in the new VW bus for Seattle and Sean, who was seven days old, and I flew to meet them there. Jack needed to be in Juneau to teach classes for a new program about fisheries, so he boarded a flight for Alaska.

I drove the van and the boys to Vancouver and then put the van on a ferry. From Vancouver, the boys and I flew in a Drumman Goose to Juneau. That was an exciting flight because we splashed down like a goose (hmmm, think that's why it got that name?) and landed on the water at cities along the flight path.

The first night in Juneau, we stayed in the best hotel (Jack told us that). There were cockroaches scurrying all over when the lights went on and no means for me to get rid of them! I hustled the boys off to bed so we couldn't see the bugs. When his evening class was finished, Jack returned and for the first time our entire family was together in our new state of Alaska.

After Jack's class the next day, we moved into a small house in the city of Douglas. (Douglas is just across the bridge over the Gastineau Channel from Juneau.) In 1963, Douglas was a small town. However, now it has grown very large because Juneau is the capital of Alaska. Both of these cities are located at the foot of mountain ranges and any room for more houses must be found farther up the side of the mountains.

Jack started the program for teaching commercial fishermen all the laws, good and practical ideas, and all the needed information about commercial fishing. He traveled to villages all over Alaska. Interest was great and class enrollment grew. As this happened, Jack traveled with men who taught motor, engine, and net repairs. The fishermen were taught how to keep records because fishing laws prohibited catching during certain hours and days and part of each season. Jack bought a 40-foot purse seiner named "Tommy Boy" and moored it in the Juneau harbor, planning to commercial fish with it in season.

Because I had worked to help our family financially while Jack earned his degrees, the plan was to have me stay at home and be mom to the boys in our new state. Living in Alaska was Jack's big dream that came true, and he was the love of my life, so that was where our hearts were.

Jack had no more than left to work on his new program when Sean came down with roseola, which I thought was measles. Sean was bright red all over and these symptoms caused me to seek medical help. I chose the Juneau group, the largest clinic with three doctors. I proudly signed papers listing my occupation as housewife/mother and former X-ray technician. When reading the completed form, Dr. Henry became excited and even held off examining Sean as he explained how badly the medical staff needed a technician at the Catholic/Native Hospital. I was told that even four hours a day would be great for the community since there hadn't been a technician on staff for six months. I accepted the job offer and was able to start the next day because a neighbor had fallen in love with our boys and would care for our two youngest along with her sons at her home.

The X-ray department was a disaster. It was clean but proper marking, labeling, and filing were a mess. Both clinic staffs were very happy to have me join them and soon I was doing 24-hour call work. The Night Calls meant waking the boys, leaving their pajamas on, and taking them to the Sisters, who worked in the nursery of the hospital. Greg thought this was great; the boys played, read, and ate with all of the Sisters' attention. I couldn't reach Jack to ask him about the job and we didn't use long distance much because of the cost. (A call to Wisconsin was $25 for three minutes.)

Some of you may be old enough to remember the Good Friday earthquake in Alaska on March 27, 1964. Cities along the fault line not only broke up and sloughed land into the ocean but also burned to the ground and suffered severe quake damage.

We had been living in Douglas for three months when the quake occurred on March 27. I was finishing up my shift in the X-ray department in Juneau when Jack surprised me by coming down the hallway and swatting a big love tap on my bottom. Not realizing that it was Jack, I was about ready to turn and let him know that he couldn't do that to me. Instead I just cried and fell into Jack's arms. I was happy to see him.

Later that evening, we went with two couples (La Bues and Friths) from our little church to attend a citywide concert of the "Seven Last Words of Christ." It was held at the biggest church in Juneau, located just across the street from the Coast Guard building. As the choir was finishing up with organ sound effects and lights that flickered on and off like thunder and lightning for the crucifixion scene, we saw the men in the back row whispering and fretting about what they heard coming through the organ frequencies: Seward was burning, Valdez was sliding into the ocean, the Anchorage area of Turnigan Arm had sloughed off into the ocean, and many houses and buildings were ruined. Oil tanks in Seward and Valdez were on fire. In Anchorage, the hotel where Jack usually stayed cracked widely down its middle and guests had to be evacuated. What a great miracle to have Jack at home on that day!

After the concert, instead of having coffee, the Friths went home with the phone numbers for my parents and Jack's mom so that L.V. could contact them by short wave. L.V. was in the Coast Guard and knew he would be called into work shortly. Jim and Katie's two children were at our place with a sitter and already sleeping, so we just stayed up eating, drinking coffee, and listening to the radio all night. As we listened, I took notes about what was happening: names of those who were found and those missing, where John was, where Mary was, where they needed baby formula and canned goods, and so on.

One hundred fifteen people died due to the destruction and the effects of water waves. It was a miracle that more people weren't killed during the quake. Nearly all of the stores were closed because it occurred on Good Friday at 5:36 p.m., a time when most of the going-home traffic had cleared, making the death toll alarming, yet not as horrific as it could have been. The two airports in Anchorage had runway damage so the medical emergencies group from Juneau and Douglas couldn't take off to go and assist. I was asked to stay in Juneau to help because Anchorage had enough technicians to cover their two hospitals. The channel between Juneau and Douglas had a 15-foot tidal drop shortly after the quake so the marinas had many problems with the boats. A 1964 *National Geographic* issue printed a long article with many photos on the earthquake destruction.

Shortly after the earthquake, I met Virginia Post, who was very kind to me. She mentioned she and her husband had a place we could rent. Her husband, Eli, who had been a miner in one of the gold mines, was always quite sick with complications of cancer. He had a fabulous garden built up to thigh height, which made it possible for him to sit on the edge to weed and arrange plants. Eli trapped for years and he and Ginnie also hunted. Virginia and Eli knew I loved the "Three Bears" rugs on their living room wall. Several years later when Eli had died, Ginnie told me that I could have the big rug if I would pay for shipping. (By that time the boys and I were living in one of my folks' duplexes in Wisconsin.) The Post's also owned a cabin on Mt. Bradley that the Chet Mattsons bought after Eli died.

Jack and I accepted Virginia Post's offer and lived in their rental house for about a year. During that time, we experienced very strong "Taku" winds from the east that rushed down the Juneau mountains and charged up Mt. Roberts behind us. The Post house was small and very cold, having little insulation in the walls. To stop the cold drafts, I stuffed the gaps around the windows with rags and put duct tape over all of the holes to seal them. Having an oil stove to cook on in the kitchen and another big brown stove in the living room for heat, I placed Greg and Doug in sleeping bags on the living room couches and a pile of their clothes right next to them in case we ever had a fire. Our bedroom was small and Sean's crib stood in it just around the corner from the stove. Our VW was parked right outside the entrance door if needed.

The strong winds also caused a lot of power outages. Whenever that happened, our friends would come over for a warm, delicious meal of blueberry sourdough pancakes. Our friends would bring their sourdough starter because we had the oil stove to cook on and keep everybody as warm as possible.

The huge snowdrifts around the Post house made a wonderful playground for the boys! One winter day when Doug and Greg were outside, walking across the top of the snowdrifts, Doug suddenly fell through the crusted snow and disappeared. Greg yelled at me to come get Doug! I ran outside. I could hear Doug calling, "Help! Help!" but I couldn't reach him. I grabbed the shovel and carefully dug into the huge drift. After his quick rescue, Doug and his brother continued to shovel into the drift to build a great tunnel. I kept a close eye on them for fear they might all get buried inside. The boys liked how the tunnel sheltered them like an igloo; however, I knew it was too dangerous to trust. Even though it seemed as if God were taking care of the boys, we caused the tunnel to cave in.

The Post house—very cold in winter; huge drifts of snow for Greg and Doug to climb

At Grampa Harry and Gramma Ruth's place in New Richmond for Christmas; Sean only four days old

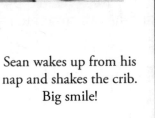

Sean wakes up from his nap and shakes the crib. Big smile!

Greg, Sean, and Doug

Chapter 6

OUR BIG, BEAUTIFUL HOME

knew Jack would be traveling around Alaska for years to promote his research. He built the program to reach villagers with knowledge of commercial fishing. He had a great plan, so I was on board. Our friends the Thorstensens were moving "out the road" and wondered if we would like to purchase their home. We sure did! Their lovely house was newer, warmer, and bigger than the Post house we were renting. (From that property, there were marvelous views of the Gastineau Channel, majestic mountains and ridges, and of Juneau in the distance stretched across the base of Mt. Roberts about three miles north.) The house had five bedrooms, making it possible for Jack to convert one room for his office. Two huge windows in the front of the house provided a stunning view of the mountains, water and snow slides in the spring, mountain goats, and many kinds of birds. The tour boats would dump their garbage along the channel and the birds had a feast.

The sale of this property seemed to fall into my lap, and I was excited about this possibility because I still saw us permanently living in Alaska. I did the pursuing for the purchase and Jack and I bought our first house. We were acquainted with the sellers of the property because they attended the same Methodist church as we did and their sons baby-sat for me at times.

So that I could go to the hospital at any time of the night to X-ray a patient, I had one or two teachers (Cathy and Sue) boarding with us. This arrangement worked well because Jack was away for work a lot of the time.

Our house was situated on a steep hill. The older boys, Greg and Douglas, enjoyed the beach below when the tide was out. Playing ball was impossible as everything rolled down the hill, but sledding and tobogganing was great fun. The boys camped on the hill in all kinds of good weather. The old Tredwell Gold Mine had been closed for many years and was off limits to my young boys, but now, grown up, my sons still talk about the things that they did when we lived in this house in Alaska.

Sean was the cutest little boy; his dark brown eyes, blond hair, and a sweet smile went over well everywhere we went. Sean was always alert and happy, especially when he woke up from his naps. He would stand and shake his crib until I got him up and out! My friend Esther played with Sean at church and told him polar bear stories and called him "Seanie Baby." Eventually he called her "Esther Baby."

As the boys all grew into longer play times, the beach was the attraction for them. We did a lot of beach combing and collected shells that were used for creating crafts.

When we went berry picking, we didn't see any bears. I was told to make a lot of noise when we went after the berries, so we all did. I used the berries to make delicious jams and jellies!

The boys and I would also travel around the area to a lot of different places. When we went hiking, Sean was carried in a pack on my back. (I'm sorry that I don't have a picture of this.) Usually, we piled into our VW bus to travel, except for the time when I loaned it to the La Bau family. They were driving north into the interior for a vacation and left me with their VW bug. (The La Baus are "forever friends" who came to visit us in Minnesota several times. Of course, whenever I traveled back to Anchorage we saw each other, too!)

I painted the exterior of the house, which is hard to believe today because I don't do well with heights. During that time, Doug learned to ride a boy bicycle and I painted it gold and black to match the house because I had extra paint. Some of our favorite trips were traveling to the airport to pick up Jack, so the boys would have their dad around for a few days. When Jack was at home, I washed his dirty clothes and cooked meals for him while he caught up with his mail. We never went out to eat because Jack ate out most of the time when he was on the road. I did "whine" a bit and wished for any kind of date with him. At that time, I was oblivious about what Jack did when he traveled. My sons' needs, my X-ray job, and the upkeep of our nice big home kept me busy.

Once, my folks flew up to visit us for a week and Dad went fishing during the Salmon Derby with L.V. and Don Fisher on Don's boat. Great memories! Jack supplied us with a lot of pink salmon and I traded that with friends for all kinds of other meat. Mom couldn't believe the food that went through our kitchen— goat, moose, deer, and caribou, any kind of salmon, and a big king crab that was still alive when Jack laid it on the kitchen floor while my folks were with us. Linus, a super nice doggie dog for a pet, couldn't deal with the crab scooting around. Linus wouldn't stop barking!

That summer I asked one of my special teenage cousins, Doris Ann, to come and baby-sit for us. What a blessing she was! Doris Ann was not only a great caregiver, but she also fit in with the youth group from church and joined many of their activities at the church camp. Actually, she was very fond of "Jim" and at one time she told me that I was harder on her than her mom! (Yes, I was overprotective.)

As homeowners, we were outfitted with shovels, a mower, ladders, and necessary equipment to care for our house and property. We still had the beginnings of some hollow core doors for furniture. A large sheet of plywood was stored under our mattress for use in an emergency if one of the big windows broke during the Taku winds. Sometimes, I applied filament tape over both of the big windows in crisscross and back and forth patterns. As the

Taku winds flexed the glass, I was so thankful that we didn't have cracks or breaks in the windows. When we lost electricity, we just didn't have it for days!

One particular night, the noises around the house were frightening me. I needed to find out what was happening outside, so I grabbed a flashlight, carried Douglas in my arms as he slept, and checked the three doors and all of the windows. Live wires were spitting and snapping around the yard to the south of the house! I couldn't phone out, but when it was light outside I made sure that we didn't go near the wires. Did I think a little boy could protect me? I felt very ashamed when I realized what I had done because of my own fear. That incident helped me get over the fear of darkness.

In the wintertime, the boys walked to school in the dark and came home in the dark. The strong Taku winds were extremely powerful. People told me to teach the boys to run for the nearest pole, wrap their arms around it, and hang on tightly if the winds came up suddenly. In the summertime, it was hard to go to bed because the sun didn't set until around 10:30 to 11 p.m. I had to add black linings to the bedroom curtains to block the light so that it would seem like night. Pretending was okay, too.

I continued to work at the hospital and finally asked for a raise because I was earning the same wage that I had been paid in Seattle. I wanted to be compensated for the 24-hour call service. If a raise was not possible, I had decided that I would quit and they could hire someone else. I remember my talk with Mother Superior (a young woman with a stocky build and serious expression). Even though I had never gone up against a Mother Superior before, I held my ground and was given a raise. The laboratory tech also handled 24-hour calls and received a good raise, too. Most of the calls related to surgery required both of us there, working.

The boys and I were alone most of the time while Jack traveled for his work! Beside beach combing (which they loved to do), we collected and dried starfish, did a lot of exploring in and out of the national forest, and hiked up mountainsides. With Sean riding in a pack on my back, Greg (age seven), Doug (age four) and I climbed Mount Roberts (3, 819 foot peak, just east of Juneau) on a beautiful summer day. On a very cold winter day, we hiked up to the ski jump on Mount Jumbo (which rises across the channel from Juneau). The boys and I also collected pinecones and acorns for craft projects, traveled out the road for group play or picnics, dug clams (which they loved to eat), and picked any variety of berries that were in season.

Our first family photograph was taken for our Christmas cards that year when we bought our first home. Little did I know that the picture would be the first and last family photo of us.

I am thankful for the way my parents raised me—to be strong, kind, faithful, and happy serving others and to be the best wife and mother possible. My parents were great role models that encouraged and inspired me. I knew "God was for me," but I didn't know about having a personal relationship with Him. That would come later.

The five bedroom house painted gold with
black trim; Doug on his "new" used bicycle

The last Doyle family photo for their
Christmas card

Chapter 7

THE END OF A DREAM

When Douglas needed to have his tonsils removed, Jack wanted to be there. So, I scheduled the surgery to coincide with Jack's next stay at home. He came to the house to pick up his mail, left for work, and then showed up at the hospital after the surgery. Jack never did come home that night. I had no idea what was happening. It was hard not to be upset because I had arranged the surgery around Jack's schedule. Trying to reach Jack, I called the college registrar (Mary) who was Don's wife, visited with her a bit, and then left a message for Jack to call me. Cell phones were not in use at that time!

The next day I checked on Doug a few time while working, and then I spent time with him until I left the hospital to pick up Greg from school. After supper, I returned to the hospital.

When I arrived, I found Jack visiting with Doug. He hardly looked at me. When I went to kiss and hug him, he turned away. "Hey," I asked him, "are you okay, Hon?"

"Oh, yah" was his answer. Doug was my concern. I fed him a gelatin snack before his bedtime and talked to him, trying to conceal any problem between his dad and me. Douglas was a wonderful little boy, very aware of my needs. He still perceives changes even today, many years later. Doug did well for the second day after the surgery and experienced no complications. I promised him that the sore throat would go away and his ears wouldn't hurt as much. The nursing Sisters had assured him and me that they would take very good care of him that night and told me to stop back in when I arrived for work in the morning.

As I prepared to depart, I could tell that Jack wasn't going to leave with me. So I asked him to come down the hallway a bit. I had our only vehicle, the VW bus, and found out that he was driving a University vehicle. While we stood in the hallway, I asked him with tears in my eyes, "What's going on? You are acting very strange for my husband who has been gone a long time. You can't even hug me when you get to come home."

I continued, "Do you realize how much I miss having you around and then you don't call or write? Most of the time I have no idea where you might be." He didn't seem to want to answer or defend himself and I assured him I certainly had a right to know what was happening.

"Are you coming home?"

"No, I will stay a little longer with Douglas."

"Well, Douglas is going down for the night right now, so perhaps we should both go home and talk about us!"

He said he would talk to me the next day. Since he didn't know much about what was going on in my life, I walked away, letting him figure out when he could find time to talk. Yes, I cried myself to sleep that night if I even did sleep and began to assess the communications we had exchanged during previous weeks.

I was loving, kind, and interested in his teaching program and I could be sexy, too! I felt I needed intimacy with him whether he did or not. Because of his occasional traveling with a guy or two I had wondered if they could possibly have feelings for each other.

The next morning before dropping Sean off at Jean's house and Greg at school, I searched through Jack's clothes in our closet and the papers on his desk. I wasn't pretending to be a detective, but I sure wanted to learn of anything that might help me understand. I found nothing but the name "Ann" and a stateside phone number on a piece of paper.

For all of these reasons—well, these few—I felt my world was falling apart. We had finally fulfilled Jack's goals and I was content living in Alaska, having him come and go for his job. After all we had been through, it seemed he didn't need me anymore!

Jack hadn't been the greatest father because he was gone so much. When he was working in Juneau and wanted the boys to go with him on his boat, they waited excitedly in their life jackets, but he didn't come.

While Douglas was still recuperating at the hospital, I was called in for X-ray work one evening. I took Greg and Sean to stay with the Sisters, knowing they would let the boys see Douglas.

We passed Clancey's house down our street and Jack's University vehicle was there. That meant he was killing time and drinking with the guy who lived there. At the hospital, the boys were glad to see each other. Soon we were heading home, knowing Doug could come home the next day after my four hours of work. Before leaving, I made it clear to the Sisters that if Jack came to take Doug home he should be told that arrangements had been made to discharge Doug with his mother. This plan was okay by the Sisters and good timing for me.

Jack called later that evening. I suggested that he should come home and be a husband and a father. I had already been in bed, but got up to freshen up, smell good, and look my best. I didn't have a good relationship or prayer life with God, but I did consider myself a Christian even though I had no right or grounds to base it on. If singing in the choir and teaching Sunday school helped, I had that going for me. I remember begging God for His help: "Please, please, please, God."

Jack walked in the door about 11 p.m. He didn't have good news or nice answers for me. He profoundly stated he didn't love me anymore. What a stab to my heart that message was! "Why?" I asked. He told me that he just didn't.

"Well, could it be because you hardly see us anymore? Is there someone else?"

"No" was his answer.

"Then, you should have a good explanation," I retorted. Our conversation went NO WHERE! I begged him and said, "I still love you." Sadly, his actions showed me that he no longer loved me. He seemed to have "left" me. At times, I'm sorry I pressed for answers that night, but then I remember how Jack acted towards me.

Jack's leaving was impossible for me to comprehend. I was still a great gal with an abundance of love overflowing from my heart. This did not dry up. My heartbreak was the result of Jack's empty feelings for me.

The boys and I didn't see Jack for a while after he gathered more of his things and left that night. Mary called about something of his and informed me that Jack was still in town. With that news, my whole world crashed into many pieces. I was the one to face family and friends. I remember thinking that I just needed to be all "mom" and X-ray technician at the hospital each day.

Jack deceived me. I remember asking myself, "Why? How could he do this to me and our sons? Why didn't he need us? Why, God?" I tried to do my very best for Jack, but after his news I wanted to hate him! I loved Jack for fourteen years, but his revelation exploded like a bomb in my heart. I had no training for handling my raw emotions. I fell to the bottom of a deep, dark pit of depression. My heart was broken! I wondered what people were going to say. What would my relatives think?

My whole insides were roaring and stressing over a series of "what-ifs" and "whys." I had thoughts of "wonder if" and plans of weird and serious "stuff." (Years later, I learned that God puts our tears in bottles, according to Psalm 56:8.)

I tried to remember the happy times and really did want to be there for my sons and shelter them from feelings of despair. I also thought my parents would love the boys so I began to plan my way out of that dark time.

God knew the situation I was in and surprised me with a visit from our friend Doyne, known as "Red" for his red hair. He was a calm, sensitive, and caring fellow. Each evening for over a week, Red came over to the house after work and ate supper with the boys and me. He was one of Jack's co-workers in the Juneau college offices. Red told me that he had heard that Jack was lunching frequently with someone who flies a lot. The woman was married. I met her once at our airport. She was a stewardess named Mrs. Peterson, whom Jack had flown with. I couldn't believe it, but I later learned that she had a sister named Ann living in the lower states.

Red became a listening friend offering encouragement that kept me from falling apart. We had no sexual attachments and I could talk about anything with him. A genius in saltwater fishing research, Red was in the process of writing an informative book on that topic. Many years later while staying at Douglas' home in Anchorage during a visit, I was able to read Red's book *(Field Guide to Alaska Salt Water Fishery,* copyright, 1985).

My friendship with Red was another miracle from God because I had made a plan for ending my life. I traveled across the high bridge between Juneau and North Douglas to get to the hospital when on call. If I finished my shift late at night, I knew I could easily park in the middle of the bridge and end my life. The light traffic would be drinkers heading home after the bars closed. I remember thinking that if something were to happen to me, my folks would rescue and care for my sons!

In the distance across the Gastineau Channel is the Juneau-Douglas Bridge that Clarice planned to jump from to end her life and marriage problems. Juneau is nestled along the channel. The mountain above the tour boats is Mt. Roberts, which Greg (age seven), Doug (age four), and Clarice climbed with Sean riding in a pack on her back on a long, summer day. The dark shaded area on the left in the foreground is part of Mt. Jumbo or Bradley. Clarice and her boys climbed this mountain on a winter day and only hiked up to the ski jump because it was very cold.
(Photo by Jim LaBau)

Chapter 8

THE BRIDGE TO NEW BEGINNING

God certainly knew where I was and had his way with me as I sat on the railing of the high bridge between Juneau and North Douglas late one night. Gripping the upright girder tightly with my left arm, I hollered out, "God, I don't hate you. I just don't want to live! I don't want to live. Oh, God, let me die!"

I sized up the distance from each shore to the water directly below and then wondered if the icy waters would cause hypothermia. Questions swirled in my head: "Who would find me? Would the police be the ones to take my car home?" I thought that Cathy and Sue would have to help with any problems at the house.

Within seconds, the words "don't jump in a dress because" popped out of the recesses of my mind—a flashback from a Red Cross Swimming lesson. I remembered when my instructor, Kirby, told the class that if a woman planned to commit suicide by jumping off a bridge, she shouldn't do it in a dress because it would billow out, cushioning the blow, keeping the person from drowning. Well, there I was sitting on the railing, wearing a surgical gown and thinking that I couldn't jump because it might billow out and cushion my blow! I had not thought about that comment for years. God brought it out of a little spot in my brain because He knew I would go to hell that night if I did jump. I was no longer a strong swimmer and the cold channel water came from glacial ice, so I probably wouldn't have made it to land on either side of the channel. What a failure! I couldn't even kill myself!

I headed home. Being the land of the midnight sun, it was still light out around 2 a.m. when I walked up to the house. I couldn't sleep with so much on my mind. I stayed up with a drink, thought about everything, and shed zillions of tears. God knew about every teardrop I shed, but I still didn't grasp how much the God of the universe, the God of creation wanted to be "MY" God as well. What a great miracle!

I thought a lot about my boys. I knew young Sean (who was four years old) still needed me because I was with him the most. My other sons were busy in school. Doug was attending kindergarten and Greg was in second grade. I really didn't have to work at the hospital. I realized I could be the best mom possible for my three sons even if I couldn't be Jack's wife!

A few days later, I met with Katie and Jim, my best friends from church—whose support I greatly appreciated and needed—and shared about my relationship with Jack. They hoped we could get marriage counseling.

Mary and Don also became closer friends and Don got me drinking scotch on the rocks, thinking I wouldn't have hangovers. They both knew what Jack was up to and yet when I questioned them, they just gave vague answers. Mary knew or could find out Jack's work schedule and where he was teaching.

I did not tell other people that I had tried to jump off the bridge. It still hadn't been completely ruled out. I was concerned that other people would turn me in as a medical case and I was determined to prevent that from happening. Even though I still worked four-hour shifts and handled on-call requests, living was difficult. I really didn't eat, didn't get a lot of sleep, and drank too much when I was at home—the deep sadness and emptiness was too painful!

While all of this was going on, I received a phone call from Jack's only brother, who lived in Milwaukee. He told me that their dad (Thomas) was dying and if Jack wanted to see him alive, he should get there as soon as possible. Jack's folks had been divorced since he was a young boy. Even though I knew very little about his father, my heart went out to Jack and felt he should travel to Milwaukee if possible. I checked our bank account and decided we could only afford to have Jack fly round trip. Once again, I did my detective work and called the Westward Hotel where Jack stayed when based in Anchorage. He wasn't registered there nor at the fisheries office at the University in Anchorage where he also had a desk. When I called the University, the secretary needed to know who I was and why I was calling before she told me that she thought Jack was taking care of a friend's cat and gave me the number to call. Even though I didn't know whose number I was calling, I left a message about an emergency in his family. He called back, angry that I had traced him. Jack decided not to travel to Wisconsin. His father died and his mother and brother were upset with me and angry that I had not reached Jack in time. I wasn't ready to tell them more; they could just be mad at me for a while. I started to think that Jack might be cheating on me when I heard the message that he was caring for some woman's cat.

Late one night after I had gone to bed, Jack called and spoke kindly to me. I couldn't help but wonder what was coming. This was a long distance visit for us; however, because I was hurting deeply, I didn't want to say, "I love you," before hanging up. I kept waiting for Jack to say more or "good-bye." Finally before ending the conversation, he said, "I love you," and I replied, "Oh, Jack, do something about it if you really do because I love you! We could do marriage counseling. What do you think?" He said he would call me and then we told each other "good-bye" and again I said, "I love you." Following that call, many more lonely nights were spent crying myself to sleep.

Life marched on for me with no future plans. Katie told me that no one would know what was happening in my life because I acted the same as usual. Actually, no one around me knew what Jack even looked like. Katie and Jim were buffers for me when it came to church and school events. Likewise, co-workers at the hospital never knew or needed to know, so I was not sure why

I felt that everyone was talking about Jack and me and that our marriage problems were now big gossip around town.

Jack finally called again to say that he had arranged a meeting with a marriage counselor and told me when I should be in Anchorage. Before the counseling session, I took time to sew a new dress. I had lost a lot of weight and was down to 135 pounds, which made me feel better about myself. (I was a very sad, hot-looking gal!) I also made plans to have Jim and Katie and their children stay in our house with the boys for about three days because we had more room. The children always enjoyed spending time with each other. We also traded cars because they drove a VW "Bug" and there would be seven of them in our "bus."

I flew to Anchorage and Jack met me at the airport and took me to lunch before our appointment. We tried to visit amicably. The conversation seemed to be going pretty good. What? He even acted like a gentleman! Oh my, he opened the doors for me—OK! When we were finally seated in the counselor's office, I heard the sound of a snap coming from under the desk and figured that a microphone was being used to record the conversation.

For a long time, the counselor asked many questions. Then, he dropped a bombshell! He asked if I thought I could be a mistress for Mr. Doyle. My response was almost verbatim, "A mistress! I wasn't brought up to be anyone's mistress! My parents raised me to be a faithful wife. What happened to that? What had I done to kill our marriage?" Shortly after that point in the conversation, I was excused by the counselor and told that he'd like Mr. Doyle to stay longer. Jack asked me to wait for him. That counselor was no help to me at all. Afterwards, Jack and I had dinner together and tried to talk about anything, I guess. This wasn't a hate issue. Instead, I was walking down the road of life with a broken, smashed, and empty heart—not knowing where to go from there. (I couldn't forgive Jack for a long time.) I tried to stay strong and not collapse into depression, which would be of no good for the core of our little family.

The next morning, I flew back to Douglas, Alaska. Later, I shared my thoughts about everything with Katie and Jim, who were a tremendous support to me and I was grateful for it. I realized that due to the traveling Jack did, he could have had a sexy mistress in more than one village.

For the boys and myself, the past eleven years had been a time of working toward everything Jack had wanted—his goals, his degrees, when he wanted them, and even where he wanted to work. Oh, how quickly my life changed! Everything was coming down like an avalanche and the boys and I were underneath it. Jack was at the top kicking the snow to make sure it all came down.

During our years of marriage, I buried the negative things "under the carpet." But when looking back, I could also see how God had blessed me with three wonderful sons and how much I enjoyed spending time with them, teaching them to talk and walk; ride bikes; build sand castles, forts, and snowmen; go on picnics; and love each other.

While I was reeling from a broken heart, Greg had started to let his studies slide and showed a listless attitude in class, which prompted me to meet with his teacher. I confided in her about some marriage concerns and acknowledged that Greg may have sensed some of those things and I would do my best to help him.

The next day, Greg's teacher took it upon herself to talk to Greg after school and told him that his parents were going to go through a divorce and that he could come to her as his friend if he ever needed to talk about his feelings. Greg came home a little late crying. We went into my bedroom where I could hear him out. Oh my, he started pounding and hitting me and telling me that his teacher told him we were getting a divorce. I was shocked! I wasn't prepared to work through any of this yet. We hugged a long time and then I told him why some of the things were happening. Crying again, he explained how he couldn't find our house and had walked right by it.

Doug became extremely quiet and I decided I should tell him some of the things and keep the conversation as "careful" as possible. He has always been more calm, quiet, and somewhat pensive than the rest of us. As an adult when he says something or speaks up, it is with more sense or wisdom than most of us say—very thought out!

What a terrible load my adorable young sons were carrying. I was blessed to be their mom and tried to lighten some of their loads. Those conversations with Greg and Doug caused me to resign from my position at the hospital and spend more time at home being THEIR MOM.

Jack, the love of my life, traveled and was gone a lot, first while serving in the Army and then during summers while working in fishery, researching in Alaska. He was the one I trusted, and together we had planned that I would support the family while he earned his degrees. We moved to Alaska to live where Jack worked and then he chose to love a stewardess. What a devastating time that was for the boys and me!

In February of 1967, Jack and I became divorced. I sold the house with no problems. Actually when the news went around the community that my sons and I were moving, someone came quickly to see and buy the house. The couple who bought the house were sweet people.

Jack's mother was very angry with him at first and told me to get everything that I could from him. (Like what did I need? I couldn't have his love.) Later she wrote to say that she would like me to return the kerosene lamp that she gave to me at my bridal shower. So that request was included in the divorce decree. I certainly didn't have a brain for all of this, but I tried to start each day, one at a time, taking one step at a time. Looking back, I realize how the boys and I were sheltered and comforted by the Lord whether I knew it or not, even when I thought I was alone.

Preparations had to be made for moving back to Wisconsin. To ship our belongings to New Richmond, I ordered a good-sized pod and had it loaded. A lot of packing was done and a lot of tears were shed!

No longer employed at the hospital, I read with interest that there was a need for locals to wear vintage costumes and meet the tour boats that arrived in Juneau, giving tourists a big welcome and taking their pictures with Polaroid cameras. It was Alaska's Purchase Centennial and for all the tourists we represented a "sourdough" or one originally born in Alaska. I decided this was something the boys and I could do. The Chamber of Commerce gave us plenty of Polaroid film to use. I wore a sexy dress, which I had whipped up to look like a "Miss Kitty" dress by remaking the bridesmaid dress I wore in Winnie and Roger's wedding in 1955. I also sewed a leather bag for storing "gold nuggets." The boys gathered small stones and spray painted them gold. I even came up with the idea to dress the boys in little gentlemen outfits. Wearing vests, white shirts, armbands, and bowler hats, my sons were as cute as could be as they gave a "nugget" to each tourist. The Tourist Center gave me a big stack of brochures to share. This was a light-hearted time as we met tourists on several weekends. Some would point and stare at us. (The boys also wore the outfits when we traveled on the airplane and met my dad at the Minneapolis airport. This made it easier to say our many good-byes when we departed from Alaska on June 28th.)

Finally, the day came when everything was finished for the move and we were ready to travel to Wisconsin. Earlier that day before the flight, Pastor Ernie and Rachel Jones gave us a great family luncheon birthday party in costume because it was Greg's birthday. After the party, they took us to the airport. Our church family really turned out for us. While taking photos in the terminal, Bea noticed that Alaska's Governor Hickle would be on the same departing flight and asked if he would be in a photo with us. Of course, he agreed and also received a gold nugget from the boys and a brochure about his state. Our thank you from him was a big smile and good wishes. Jack was also there to say good-bye, hug the boys, and pose for a photo.

Other travelers in the airport and on the flight stared at us, but I didn't care. We were starting a new life near our best and bigger family! Sean (four-years old) got very sick during the descent. As passengers were disembarking in Minneapolis, my dad thought we might not be on the flight because we were the last ones off. Sean hadn't given me time to get the urp bag out of the seat pocket. We had stayed behind so I could help the stewardess clean up our mess.

On the drive to Wisconsin, Dad stopped at my sister Winnie's house so we could receive more hugs and love. Winnie recognized the material in my gay 90's dress and, of course, more pictures were taken of my family. While we were gathered outside of Winnie's house, Becky—a red-haired, ten-year-old, neighbor girl—walked by and stood looking at us, probably wondering what was going on. (We actually did see her again in our lives.) We could have given her some gold nuggets and a brochure, but we were very excited. This was the beginning of many hugs and love for us. The boys and I were celebrating! Happy tears! My dad's love for us was more than I could hope for. He watched me while holding Sean or standing by one of the boys. Happy day!

When we finally arrived at my folks' house, Mom was already at home after a full day of teaching and Bev's and Butch's families arrived shortly to welcome us. The warmth of their love felt really good. This was a dream come true—to be loved again by close family.

Our new beginning felt safe and comfortable; I was mom to my sons, surrounded by relatives and new friends who loved us. The boys and I stayed with my folks until the pod with our belongings arrived and then we moved into a duplex close to my folks' house. I truly felt God blessing us and there was a desire in my heart to know more about Him, but I hadn't figured out how that was possible.

Governor Walter Hickle with Clarice and the boys (costumed for Alaska's 100th birthday); departed on the same flight out of Juneau in 1967

Chapter 9

NEW IN NEW RICHMOND

*B*eing totally alone with the boys all the time was not something I saw coming. I knew I couldn't afford to live in Alaska as a single mom because of the high cost of living and the cost of travel for four of us. I also certainly didn't want to take in Jack's mail and dirty laundry so he could come take an occasional peek at the boys and me for the rest of our lives.

It was a relief to be living near my folks and new friends in New Richmond, Wisconsin on the widespread of the Willow River. Dad and Mom owned some homes that Dad built to rent or sell. One of them was a two-level duplex and its lower walkout was ready for the boys and me to move into. The pod arrived with enough belongings to set up our new home nicely. Dad had built a bunk bed in the pump room so that Greg had a small, uniquely different room of his own.

While married to Jack, perhaps I was a bit gullible and a romanticist, focusing on our future plans and trusting each other while we were apart. After the divorce, I found myself grieving over the loss of hope. Loss of Jack. Loss of togetherness. Loss of LOVE and romance. There was a big hole in my heart and I had to deal with problems for the four of us. So, I cried in my pillow only at night! I was determined to be with the boys a lot for their security, filling their empty emotional spaces and keeping them interested in the new things around us.

Time seemed to help me if I let it. I wasn't trusting God for direction in my life, but instead I tried to provide for all of my family's needs and fix the problems myself. Days and nights rolled into each other. I continued to loose weight and my aunts and uncles would drop in to see how "terrible" I looked. "Have you seen Clarice Mae?" My weight loss was the best thing that could have resulted from months of marriage and divorce problems. I felt my best physically at that time, even more sexy.

My folks were wonderful for giving my sons and me hugs and encouragement during that time of transition. Today, I still miss Dad and Mom very much and wish I could pick up my phone and call them at no charge. I would tell them how much I appreciate them and, of course, thank them for being special gifts from God.

Greg was a handsome ten year old, very tall for his age, and ready to handle more responsibility when we moved into the duplex. He was my "little man" to help me in many ways. He protected Douglas and was tender hearted. Greg started to mow the lawn with me overseeing. One day, he came across a nest of baby mice and brought one to me, holding it by the tail. The mouse bit his hand and he let it fly! He kept mowing for us and even began to shovel snow in the winter. Greg grew very close to Grampa Harry (my dad). They spent time together fishing, hunting, and working in my dad's shop.

Greg and Doug were enrolled in the elementary school where their Gramma Ruth was teaching students in special education classes. They rode the school bus because I thought that would help them meet more kids in our neighborhood and also prevent them from entertaining Mom before and after her classes when she needed to give full attention to her students and complete lesson preparations.

For a fun evening, Winnie and Roger occasionally took me with them when going out for a drink. That brought about men being interested in me. When some older guys were hitting on me, Winnie and Roger were shocked. They were my protection!

In the fall, I joined the Sweet Adelines group and became very involved with singing and making costumes for the nine of us. The group didn't travel but did sing for a lot of local functions.

Within a few months after we settled in the duplex, my brother, Butch, and his wife, Jo, moved back from California. It was great to see them and get our boys together socially—catch-up time!

In November, following a delicious Thanksgiving meal, my siblings and their spouses drew names for exchanging Christmas gifts. While sitting next to Jo, she showed me her suggested "want" for Christmas—"baby girl." So, I wrote on my paper—"new husband."

Being able to celebrate the Christmas season with my folks was wonderful, because my sons and I had missed many extended family holiday gatherings and special occasions. My parents created a loving and supportive environment for us. I did some cleaning and baking and made meals occasionally for them, too, which was always appreciated.

About five months after moving back from Alaska, I called Winnie in Woodbury, Minnesota to ask her to check when the Swinging Singles met and heard her say, "Oh, no!" I did not even know what swinging singles were or I wouldn't have asked! She called a neighbor's house a few blocks away and talked to Marvin, whose wife had died of cancer earlier that summer. (Winnie had told me what Marvin's family had gone through.) Anyway, he recommended that Winnie should accompany me to the singles meeting because there would be so many men present at the social gathering that I would certainly be propositioned. He described the gathering a bit and then asked, "Whom was she calling for?" and being that it was for her sister, Marvin asked, "What is she like?" Winnie told him things like I weighed 350 pounds, my hair was white, some of my teeth were broken, and I needed dental work because my former husband used to beat me up. (Oh, dear, to this line of junk!) Marvin told Winnie that he would like to meet me. "Oh sure, we will introduce you to her sometime," she replied. (She knew both of us and didn't think we were a likely pair.) "When?" he asked. They decided that Sunday evening at Winnie and Roger's house would work.

Winnie told me the plans but wouldn't reveal the name of the single man and insisted that I come to her house! I borrowed a sheath navy dress from Mom and black strap heels from Winnie and felt sort of "hot." "Go for it!" I thought.

That evening, just before Marvin arrived, Winnie finally revealed to me who was coming. When Marvin entered the house, he walked over to the colored TV set and adjusted it perfectly. Then, we met. That evening, the four of us played cards, smoked, and drank. We were interrupted when one of Marv's children called to say that the hot water heater sounded bad. Marv told the child how and where to turn it off. Later, another child called about the heater and after the third call, Marv left in a little huff to take care of it himself. Not knowing if Marv's family would have water or not, Winnie decided to fill up her largest plastic containers with water to send home with Marvin in hopes that this would carry them overnight and be enough for a morning wash up before school.

After Marvin returned to Winnie and Roger's house, I felt that I should start heading back to Wisconsin. New snow had fallen. Not wearing boots, I carried a large container of water to Marv's vehicle and followed in the tracks he made. Then, I went and sat in my car and waited until Marv moved his vehicle so I could leave.

That was an evening to mull over—thinking about the what-ifs—and trying to fall asleep. I learned that Marvin had four children: Stephen, who was fourteen years old, Rodney, who was thirteen years old, Becky, who was ten, and Paul, who was seven. They were adjusting to the loss of their mom, who had died from cancer, and to having their dad date. (Becky was the pretty, red-haired girl who stood near Winnie and Roger's house and watched my sons and me unload from my dad's car and have our pictures taken in our costumes.)

Former neighbors of Marv told me later that to get through his wife's dying, Marvin drank a lot and would show up at their place drunk in the wee hours of the morning. When I met Marv, I thought he was extremely neat and clean. I really appreciate guys with clean fingernails. (His nails were great!) He could visit with people and he loved to sing.

The following Wednesday before Marv came to my house with his friend, Bob, I prepared pumpkin pie for them. Feeling very nervous, I vacuumed the carpet a couple of times. Later, when they arrived, much to my surprise, Marv picked up a couple of little fuzzies from the floor! Of course, the guys razzed me for not buying a Wards TV from the company they worked for. (My colored TV was a Sears.)

Marvin Erickson was a minister's son and that was like one foot into heaven for me! Marvin and I began dating. He drank a lot and I did, too, when I was with him. After a couple of drawn out late night dinner dates, we began to do things together with all of the children—his and mine. (The "Prince" met the "Princess" and after much flirtation we discussed our future, our children, finances, child support, in-laws, sexualities, and a lock on the bedroom door.)

Sometimes, the expression "it's a small world" does make sense! There was one special occasion that I attended as a young girl with my family when the David Afdahl family was also there. We knew them and so did Marvin's family. In fact, Marvin was Dave's best man at Dave and Ruth's wedding. I was fourteen years old at that time and impressed with Marv's Air Force uniform (he had enlisted in the service) and how great he looked wearing it. After the wedding ceremony, I stood by and watched the wedding party mess with the bride and groom's suitcases in the trunk. Oh dear!

When Marvin and I did things together with the children, he drove a station wagon and we would all pile in! Stephen almost always rode up front with us and Doug stood on the hump right behind me, close enough to touch me or talk in my ear. Greg, Becky, and Rodney were sitting behind us and Paul and Sean were usually riding way back in the car. For one of our family dates, I wore a "frosted" wig. While we traveled in the car, Doug lifted it off my head and said, "My mom's wearing a wig!" Yes, I grabbed it and tried to get it back on as quickly as possible.

For another group date, we enjoyed ice skating and had a wiener and marshmallow roast right in front of the duplex on the wide spread of the river. The fire was built right on the ice. Having attended a lot of auctions, my dad had purchased many pairs of skates for his other grandchildren. However, that night the skates were ours to use. It behooved me to think the fire wouldn't fall right through the ice.

One unusual date was when we had the great idea that we could all learn how to ski! Dad also owned a lot of clamp-on skis for the younger kids. Stephen and Rodney had better skis. By the time we paid for their tickets, got them all outfitted, and put hats, scarves, and mittens on them, Marv and I were no longer interested in skiing ourselves. So we went inside the lodge and drank. Gradually the younger children came in without their mittens on. Doug was (and still is) very determined and followed the two older boys to the advanced slopes. While going down, he would just sit back on his skis and close his eyes! We never went skiing as a family again, but later the oldest five children went. We knew skiing would drain us financially, so we came up with other ideas for dates.

Another fun, full evening for us was to attend the Ice Capades downtown St. Paul. That was one date where we were "contained" in one place. The traffic after the Winter Carnival parade came to a standstill in super gridlock on the hill. So, Marvin turned the car off and we were kissing, kissing, kissing and the passengers around us were looking, looking, looking. The kids let us know about it. "Dad, everyone IS looking!" Perhaps the people in the other cars thought it was no wonder they had a car full of kids OR maybe they thought they should go home and kiss like that!

We certainly had many great times together on family dates. The most challenging task was determining how to discipline his or my children. It seemed like I was the one having to be the disciplinarian while Marv almost always backed off on that job. Thus, he wasn't viewed as the mean one.

Some other fond memories include the times when Marv and I and the children would visit my folks. All of us would gravitate to the player piano and sing our hearts out. Later when Marv and I were married, Dad found one for sale and we bought it. Occasionally when Marv was playing it and I answered the phone, the caller would ask, "Who is that playing the piano?" I enjoyed answering, "That's Marv!"

For one of our "alone" dates, we decided to go bowling. I had never tried bowling. Marvin was a former league bowler and wanted to get back in shape for that. He told me what was expected and showed me how to hold and release the ball in the bowling lane. We played three games and I beat him on all three and then we went home. Later, I realized I should have let Marv win so he could be the hero! It was all "beginner's luck" for me. I never bowled after that and neither did Marv!

Whenever Marvin and I spent time alone as a couple, it seemed like we compartmentalized each other and the children, but we also began to plan for the future. At the beginning of the New Year, Marv guided me down the stairs of the duplex entrance, turned around in front of me, took out a diamond ring, and asked me to be his wife. "Yes!" I answered with a kiss I can still remember. That "yes" was loaded with life experiences and emotional baggage I hadn't considered at the time and, oh, did we have a lot to learn.

One weekend before we were married, the boys and I went up to visit Marv and his kids at their house in Woodbury. Becky, who was ten years old, was making doughnuts in the deep fryer! I was appalled. I stuck close to her and encouraged her to be extremely careful with the hot grease and praised her for the skillful job she was doing. (We loved her doughnuts!)

Marvin and I wanted a small private family wedding in Marvin's church and we were married on February 24, 1968. For that special occasion, I got each child something new in clothing to wear and was especially happy for Becky because she had taken on a lot of responsibility in the house and was wearing some of her mom's clothes.

The children all looked great the day of our wedding. My dear friend, Jan, had given Becky a new hairdo. I remember thinking how beautiful Becky looked with her gorgeous red hair and new outfit, which gave her a great lift. The six boys (Stephen, Rodney, Gregory, Douglas, Paul, and Sean) looked handsome and spiffy and seemed to be excited about the day. Greg wanted to light the candles before the ceremony and that was a good job for him. The boys and some cousins also decorated my car for Marvin and me to use when we departed afterwards. Following the ceremony, we all enjoyed the delightful reception my folks hosted at their beautiful home in New Richmond.

Marv had planned a wonderful honeymoon in Orlando, Florida, where we stayed with his friends of many years who had five daughters. It was great getting to know them and seeing so many parts of Florida in the short time we were there.

In 1967, Clarice and the boys moved into the lower walkout level.
Jan and Dick lived on the main level.

Marvin and Clarice with the kids after the wedding ceremony on
February 24, 1968

Clarice's folks,
Harry and Ruth Hop

Chapter 10

MOVING INTO "THEIR" HOME

After Marvin and I returned home from our delightful honeymoon, I discovered quickly that there was no room in Marv's house for my sons and that issue became paramount. Extended family members and friends had stacked our belongings in "our" garage. We solved the problem by putting all of the boys in the long narrow bedroom with the three oldest ones together at one end and the three youngest at the other. To help out, my folks bought two sets of trundle bunks, which were moved into that room. Each boy was also given a dresser and some space in the big closet. Becky had her own room and I took my place in Marvin's bedroom. It was especially difficult for me to pack up his first wife's clothing and belongings to make room for mine.

Once each of us had a defined space I thought life for a large family would be easier. WRONG! Little did I know that most families encounter stresses and challenges when they combine two sets of children, especially those who are experiencing grief. I felt we were "nine demential." Well, I don't know when or if it did become easier. However, there were times when it was more pleasant than others. The worst and often biggest hurts for me happened when Marv's older kids said, "It is more our house than yours because we were here first." Or, when I was told, "Well, you're NOT my mother."

Everyone in the family had to work through many changes. One of the biggest adjustments for me was menu planning and food preparation. What a difference it was to make meals for nine people instead of four! I didn't grocery shop or plan meals for the month like Marvin's first wife did. In fact I learned to set the table as soon as I came in; everyone would then know we were going to eat. I tried to keep the freezer and cupboards full so I could quickly prepare a meal, even for extra guests if they dropped in. This worked most of the time. Guarding the food in the kitchen was also a full-time job especially since the two oldest sons stayed up later than Marvin and I did. I would make lunches for the kids before I went to bed and put their names and happy faces on the bags. The next morning, the kids would eat breakfast, grab their lunches, and meet their school buses right out in front of the house. In time I became familiar with each child's likes and dislikes.

The chest freezer in the basement squeaked when the top was raised. I would holler down the stairs and say, "Hey! Get out of the freezer!" Gradually the cookies and brownies "walked" away. I honestly didn't always know who was eating them, but the tins would be brought up with only one or two treats left. After

Stephen oiled the hinges, I didn't have any idea when someone snacked quietly from the freezer and I didn't get to holler either!

During this time of transition, Stephen—a handsome fourteen year old with red hair—started to case the house to see what I had changed or moved out each day. He became upset if something was missing. Stephen would, however, pitch in and help by lifting or moving heavy things when needed.

Rodney (thirteen years old) came in one day after school and exclaimed, "When are we ever going to get rid of the mess in the garage?" (Rodney liked to keep his stuff organized and took great care of his things. His baseball glove was like new!) Every time I needed to find something in my boxes, I discovered that the boxes had been changed and moved around and there would be a new maze in the garage.

The task of combining the households became mostly five-year-old Sean's and mine, as we were the ones at home. Occasionally, we would get a call from Marvin in the morning and drive to an Embers restaurant to meet him for lunch. We always seemed suspect because when Sean saw him he would call out, "Hi, Marv!" As the diners looked at us, I felt they thought we were meeting this Montgomery Wards service man on the sly and wondered if his wife knew what's going on.

Paul, the youngest of Marv's sons, was a happy and easy-to-love seven-year old, who enjoyed playing with his friends in the neighborhood. He would hop, skip, and jump even while talking to me. Paul was quick to stay close to me until I answered his questions and then he took off to play again. Any money he earned he generously shared with his friends. Paul accepted me as the mother figure in our house. A nice miracle!

Becky had been the "little mom" for their family. I wanted her to be able to play with her friends and have time for her interests, so I tried to unload her of responsibilities. I made sure that she didn't have to prepare meals unless she wanted to help.

Mom and I discussed the importance of displaying some Alaskan artifacts instead of keeping them hidden or packed away in the garage. I felt it would be good for my sons to have a touch of what they brought into the "blended family." Mom agreed and suggested using the family room in the basement. Marvin wanted to finish it off better so we filled the family room with my furniture, floats, goat and bearskins, and a Sears TV along with a pool table. This was where the kids relaxed with friends and watched television. Finally, a bit of "Alaska" was in our home.

Some of the new rules for our blended family included NO swearing, NO one saying "shut up," and NO stealing from anyone. Well, the kids tested these rules. For saying "shut up," the child had to stand against the kitchen wall and swallow a teaspoon of Tabasco sauce. Soon, those words were out of their vocabulary! Years later, my nephew Brent came with his wife to pick up some things I wanted them to have and he told her that was where he had to stand and take a teaspoon of Tabasco sauce. "No, you didn't!" I exclaimed. I guess he had been involved!

Eventually, Marv and I decided to hold a garage sale. My folks suggested that Marv's former in-laws should come the night before the sale and take things they wanted. Marvin had noticed that they had already been in his house while he was at work one day before I moved in and took things they figured they should keep. Well, they came and loaded up! It was good for us to hold this sale. Some of the kids made money selling their own things. I need to mention that Marvin and I got married in February because six of the children would be in school and it would give me some free time. Wrong! It was time alone to unpack my things and give the garage back to Marvin. God blessed me with strength, energy, and courage during that time.

Marvin and I loved having a special time "getting away from the races" at home. Many nights after supper we would take the service truck back to Ward's and Marvin would check in at the warehouse. After that, we stopped for a drink at one of his favorite places.

The task of selecting and decorating the Christmas tree was always a challenge in our household. Everyone had an opinion! I was told, "We always do it this way or we get this kind or we always buy it at the Boy Scout lot and we decorate with these ornaments or it's too short or too skinny or too big." Our first Christmas together was especially hard for me because of the disagreement. I broke down and cried it out in our bedroom—no longer caring if we had a tree. The stress of decorating for Christmas just became too much! No one came into the room to comfort me. As a result, the kids decorated the tree and I didn't have to do it. That was just about the end of tears, especially to get my way, so I think I grew up a whole lot.

The Christmas gift giving also had to be organized financially so that we didn't go into debt. Marvin and I decided not to have any credit cards other than the Wards card because we shopped for the family there using his discount.

My next goal was to have the veins in my legs stripped again, due to health reasons. This time it was a shorter stay for me in the hospital, but similar procedures were used once again. The family came to visit me and because I looked all right they couldn't tell I was sick. The children did get to see the huge aqua heaters around each leg. Try to sleep with those babies on!

We constantly needed updates or organization in the house. During the first few years as a big family, we could still burn trash and the boys had to work if they were going to live there! The older ones got the job of burning. For quite a while, the job chart was displayed on the refrigerator door. Marvin also installed hooks lower in the coat closet for the younger boys' jackets. No one was allowed to leave pairs of shoes near the entrance door because we would then have a mountain of them!

When Sean started kindergarten, the other kids attended different schools. Our school district did not provide kindergarten yet, so Sean attended a Lutheran Church school and I drove him to and fro. Paul and Doug were enrolled in the elementary school where Aunt Winnie taught, Becky and Greg were students in separate junior high schools, and Rodney and Stephen attended St. Paul Park High. There was no way I could keep up with all of their functions at five different schools and prioritizing them became necessary. We displayed a big calendar above the kitchen bar/table and by the telephone so that it could be used to help us stay organized. (I also did this in Alaska and one of my friends there would read it just to see what I had been doing.)

Our family had many special, fun times visiting Herman and Alice, who were like farm grandparents to us. Alice would put on a clean apron when we came and gave us a warm welcome. The kids really enjoyed looking for kitties in the haymow and running all over the farm and down along the banks of Rush River. The youngest boys would ride "Rosie." She became their pet cow. The older boys hiked much farther away—down to the coulee and up and down the cliffs and a sand pit. Doug spent parts of many summers there on the farm and was a big help.

Herman and Alice were wonderful, loving treasures to us and I could not conceive getting to heaven and not seeing them there. After I found Jesus, I had the blessed privilege of leading Alice to the Lord one day in her kitchen and Uncle Herman much later in his barn. They came to know that God could meet them anywhere and at all times with the promise of eternal life!

Both Marvin and I became involved in Scouting because the boys wanted to join; however, Marvin quickly lost interest. I continued to support the boys' participation through the Cub Scout and Webelos Scout programs. I loved working with costumes and really got involved when it came to their uniforms. What a joy it was to sew on the badges as the boys earned them and how proud I was of their accomplishments!

I remember when Paul wanted to earn the Cub Scout badge for climbing a tree. One day, he chose a tree that leaned over the creek at the bottom of our back hill. Without telling anyone, he shimmied up the tree and stopped about halfway, realizing that he couldn't climb back down because I would get mad at him if he got his clothes all muddy from the mud that was left on the tree from his shoes. So, he slid off the tree trunk, hanging on for dear life—like in the movies—and screaming for help—help—help! I was doing laundry in our basement and heard his plea. Recognizing Paul's voice, I called for Stephen to get to him as fast as he could, knowing if I tried to walk down the hill to the creek, I would slip and roll. Even though the water level in the creek was high at that time, Stephen waded out to reach Paul. He had Paul stand on his shoulders and then gradually walked him back to shore. Hurrah! And, Paul passed that badge assignment!

Paul loved to talk! He would entertain everyone with his exciting and imaginative stories. He could talk about anything. If you listened carefully and commented, he kept on talking so his story got longer. Paul had a very busy imagination and loved to make up games and fun things to do.

One summer, we drove Greg, Paul, and Doug to the Boy Scout camp at Rice Lake, Wisconsin. The boys had to bring self-addressed stamped envelopes to send mail back home and at least one sheet of paper to write a letter to us. Oh, how precious that letter was to me! Paul was the winner of this because it rained the first three days and he was depressed! Everything was wet! In his letter, he moaned about everything they did and asked us to come see him, send cake, and send more money. The letter arrived on Friday. (Marv and I were going to pick him up the next day.) We laughed and I also cried because I could just see him feeling lonesome and hurting and being wet.

I'm very proud of Paul because years later he graduated from the University of Minnesota-Morris, earning a B.A. degree in social and political science, and obtained a Minnesota secondary education certificate. He later worked for the Scout Council, procuring funding, etc. Now, he does similar work for a very special, beautiful hospital.

While growing up, the boys had several racetracks for different cars and played with a large quantity of GI Joe items. They also used catsup and firecrackers while playing war games on the back hill and I made burlap "sand bags," rubbery rain gear, and sleeping bags for their army. Stephen even took moving pictures of their soldiers on the hill. I think he acted the role of the general. (Stephen would also organize games in the street for the neighborhood kids. This really showed his love for kids!)

When Sean was old enough, he also joined Cub Scouts and wanted to earn his hunting small game badge for Webelos, but no older guys would take him. I kept telling him that I would take him hunting, but he didn't want me to do that. Later as a grown-up, Sean explained why I couldn't take him. It's because I wore a skirt and didn't wear jeans at all. (I had to wear heavy elastic stockings and they were always hot!)

An inexpensive fun evening of entertainment for our family was a visit to the airport to watch the airplanes land and take off at dusk. We would head up to the observation area on top of the terminal and safely watch the planes, enjoying our time together there. We often brought pop and popcorn for snacks. It was exciting for us to watch the jet brigade automatically roll out and slowly arrive or move away from the main terminal.

Through the years, we celebrated and hosted many birthday parties for the kids with their friends and then with the family. Because Sean's birthday was December 22, I made certain to celebrate on that day or it would have been forgotten and squeezed in with the exchange of gifts from under the tree. Mother Erickson would arrive on that day to stay with us for a while over the holidays. She was always unhappy with me whenever I asked her about how long she planned to stay, even though I tried to explain that any length of stay was just great and would be okay! There were always huge loads of laundry and meal preparations that had to be done for our large family. I tried to stay organized, knowing I would be doing a big wash or heading out to buy a lot of groceries or driving Mother Erickson around to visit her three brothers and sister-in-laws.

I have many memories of Mother Erickson's presence in our house. We also made about three trips a year to Moorhead to visit and help her with the yard work, garden work, and cleaning the windows and inside the house.

Our first "big family" trip to Mother Erickson's house in Moorhead is a special memory. On the way there, we stopped to visit two of Marv's first wife's aunts in Wheaton, Minnesota. What sweet ladies they were! They loved to see the children all lined up and watched them play outside after eating cookies. I was told that the women had been praying for me even if they didn't know who Marv's new wife would be and they were very happy for Marvin to have such a nice wife and family. Before that day, no one had ever talked about praying for me! I never forgot what the aunts told me. That felt so good!

Chapter 11

MEETING JESUS —I FOUND HIM!

The summer of 1970, the neighbor ladies were sending their children to Vacation Bible School at Oakdale First Baptist Church about five miles away, so I enrolled our three youngest children as well. The bus picked them all up along with Sean, Paul, and Doug right in front of our place. This was a real deal because the kids went every afternoon that week. It always amazed me how much I accomplished when even a few of the children were away from the house. After the Thursday afternoon session, Sean came in and asked me, "What color is sin, Mom?" Well, I didn't know and he said, "It is des - per - ately wicked. Who can know it?" "It's black" and off he went. It really struck me in my heart as if the Holy Spirit stabbed me Himself with conviction and I didn't know what to do.

Later, when Becky was doing the two-fingered peace sign, Sean said, "You shouldn't say that, Becky, because God is holy first." Well, our older boys liked to do the peace sign behind the younger ones for photographs. After I finally got them to STOP doing it, the younger ones would mimic them.

Throughout the week of Bible School, I had a strong desire to attend the Friday evening program. I brought the boys and stayed for the program. The children sat up straight, sang loudly, and recited verses. I was very impressed by everything, except when the pastor blew a whistle in the sanctuary. I must have thought there was a law against that.

God was also trying to reach me in other ways. Certain people would call on Marvin and me on Thursday evenings. We lied, saying, "we have a church and we love our own church" and hid our drinks behind us while they were there. When I was alone, I would search any scripture in the Bible that would help me understand God. I also noticed that the most popular bumper sticker was I FOUND IT; however, no one could tell me what was lost or what was found. That expression and the graffiti "GOD IS DEAD" bothered me all the time. I knew God couldn't be dead because He didn't let me kill myself on the bridge in Alaska. In researching those two statements, I found them to be very anti God. Friedrich Nietzsche, a German philosopher, was responsible for the words against God.

Marvin and I would double date with Elmer, a born-again friend of Marvin's from Wards, and his wife. Elmer would catch me when Marv was not nearby and say one-liners like "Jesus is waiting for you, Clare" and "You should just try Jesus." This gave me more to think about!

One very hot Thursday afternoon, Pastor Jensen stopped by for a visit. I had just stripped the family area and kitchen floor and needed to apply wax. I was wearing short shorts and got busted! I served iced tea. The doors were open so the kids ran in and out and wondered why the minister was there. Pastor Jensen told me that Sean had asked Jesus to be his Savior AND that I could as well. I responded, "Oh, yah? So, what is that all about?"

My Bible was nearby because I had been searching for peace. I had found the best and least understood message four times. It said you needed to loose your life to find it—a little different wording each time. Of course, I wasn't sure what that meant nor able find it again, but I really knew I was lost.

That afternoon Pastor Jensen explained what that message meant and showed me the verses that he called the "Roman's Road." I've used those verses many times since to share this wonderful miracle of salvation!

Here are the verses Pastor Jensen shared with me:

Romans 3:23 — For all have sinned and come short of the glory of God.

Romans 6:23 — For the wages of sin is death, but the gift of God is eternal life through Jesus Christ our Lord.

Romans 5:8 — But God commendeth his love toward us, in that, while we were yet sinners, Christ died for us.

Romans 10:9–10, 13 — That if thou shalt confess with thy mouth the Lord Jesus and shalt believe in thine heart that God hath raised Him from the dead, thou shalt be saved. For with the heart man believeth unto righteousness, and with the mouth confession is made unto salvation. For whosoever shall call upon the name of the Lord shall be saved!

Down on my knees at the couch, I did just that. I confessed my sin and asked Jesus to be my Savior. The best miracle!

I finally FOUND what I was missing. I knew it was real because my heart felt very happy. I just wanted to tell everyone. I really felt FORGIVEN! (I would have loved to pull my shorts down longer, too!) Then, Pastor Jensen helped me to put a marker in my Bible for each verse.

After the pastor left, I felt ecstatic, twirling and jumping around and wanting to tell the whole world! I clapped my hands and cried for joy! I quickly phoned the neighbor gals and Winnie and asked them to come for iced tea. As they sat around my table later that afternoon, I told them I had something really special to tell them. I started by opening my Bible to Romans 3:23 and telling them they were all sinners. As I looked up, I rushed on about the wages of our sin and what we had to do about it, and so on. Well, when I finished not one of my friends wanted my Savior and they left—a little huffy, like who was she to tell them they were sinners!

I was also eager to tell Marvin about what had happened. I prepared his favorite meal that was meatballs with mashed potatoes and mushroom gravy. I met him at the door with a big hug and a great kiss. I told him that supper was ready as soon as he washed up and that I had some very special news after we ate.

I had bookmarked his big Bible and planned to use those verses after we were done eating.

Yes, I did it all wrong again because as I shared the verses, I asked Marvin, "Did you know that was in the Bible?" "Yah," he replied. Well, Marv was a Lutheran minister's son and had probably attended more than one session of confirmation. Sharing about my faith at that time didn't work either.

I wasn't discouraged by those attempts to witness to Marv and my neighbors. My desire to grow in my faith was strong and I was fortunate to have several local Bible stations on the radio and I followed as many sermons or studies as possible. With my Bible open on the table or kitchen counter as I worked, it became more important to me to listen to the radio, than to watch the TV programs.

It wasn't long before I decided to quit drinking. Then later, I quit smoking—actually it was October 20, 1970. It was no longer a lot of fun to be with me. It didn't seem right to dance with other gals' husbands and drinking seemed such a sick waste. This meant I WAS no longer ANY FUN AT ALL!

The Bible became alive and real to me.

I learned:
- I was His witness (an ambassador) and for me to live is Christ.
- I can do all things through Christ.
- He gives us power. We should always be abounding in the work of the Lord.

- I not only had LIFE, but I could have it more abundantly!
- The Lord is my shield, my buckler, my defender.
- He shows me His path for my life.
- The Lord has a mansion prepared for me.
- I could win my husband by my conversation. (Fourteen years later the miracle happened! Praise the Lord!)
- I needed to keep my sin confessed.
- The Lord will complete a good work in me.
- I not only believe in miracles, I depend on them!
- When Jesus left the earth, He gave us His peace and His power.
- He will deliver us.

Over the years, I have recorded several lists of His promises and I'm thrilled to keep adding to them as I find more in His Word.

Chapter 12

WE ARE GROWING . . .

For six years Marvin and I had four teenagers with "hollow legs" in our house and then for one more year there were five. The teenagers kept me busy making sure there was plenty of food in the house for them! Doug was great to ask, "Can I help you?" and honed his cooking skills in the kitchen by helping me at times. I did a lot of baking for the "silent freezer" to be able to pull out snacks as needed. When we were visiting as the "group," I also tried to bring food so as not to overwhelm our loved ones. My mom always had packages of "days old" cookies that she opened for the kids to clean out. Besides that responsibility, one of my jobs was to teach all of the teenagers to drive. We would use my car because Marvin wouldn't share his. This meant the kids could occasionally drive my car after each one obtained a driver's license.

As the older boys needed more privacy, my brother built big cabinets in the basement for them to house their toys first and then other things. Later, we converted that corner into a bedroom for the two older sons.

Dating was also on the scene for our teenagers. Because there was only one phone line and two telephones with very long cords, one upstairs and one down, it was a common sight to see the cords extending throughout the house as the teenagers tried to have private conversations.

While they were young, Doug and Paul went forward to accept Christ. I was thrilled when they made their decisions. Later, Paul came to me one day and asked if his mother was in heaven already. "Oh, well, I guess we can't know that, Paul," I answered. "She was a very nice woman and a great mom, so we can hope she is." Becky overheard our conversation and said, "YES, she is!" I was curious as to how Becky knew this and asked her. Becky quickly brought out a small, white Bible that belonged to her mom—a Gideon Bible for nurses. The profession of faith was in the back, like it is in all of the Gideon Bibles. Oh, what a blessing for the kids to find this out! Their mom had written: May 14, 1945 as the day she asked Jesus to be her Savior. Her kids were satisfied. This is a great example of why it's important for us to record the date when we repent of our sins and let Jesus become our Savior.

Marv's kids lost their mom when she died at the young age of thirty-six. I was only thirty-three when I had that conversation with Paul and Becky. That really convicted me to be sold out to God, give Him my whole life, and be a bolder witness. Almost everyone I knew did not know or had not received this personal Savior. All of the churches I had attended did not teach me about salvation and the way to eternal life—only more of the "works ways." I had sung in choirs and taught Sunday School and Bible times but never learned about salvation.

Eager to learn more, I read about baptism in the Bible and was convicted about it following my salvation. I knew it wasn't any part of salvation; however, I learned that New Testament believers were quick to be baptized by immersion. So, I talked to Pastor Jenson and he set a date. I also talked to my family about being baptized and Marvin commented, "Do you want to be married or baptized?" My response was, "I hope God will make that choice for me."

About three months later, I was baptized—no big party; however, I personally felt a strength and spiritual power and boldness in witnessing to others and in my commitment to the Lord. There was a tremendous peace in my heart. I felt very "blessed" to belong to the King and have the assurance of Heaven whenever I die.

One night, as I tucked Sean into bed, he asked, "Mom, have you dedicated your life to Jesus?" I had to admit that I had not done this, even though I had accepted the gift of salvation and professed that Jesus had died on the cross for my sins. So, right then I knelt by Sean's bed and gave my whole life to Jesus. I have never forgotten about that special night. Through the years, I have recommitted my life when I felt far from my Heavenly Father's will for me.

Chapter 13

HEALTH & NEWS REPORTS

*B*ecky was hardly ever sick. However, there was one time when all of the children, except Stephen, the oldest, had a bad case of the flu. The "sick six" stayed in the bunks in one room—each one with an empty ice cream bucket in the bed. I was the busy "urppie nurse." Marv kindly hooked up one of our televisions in their bedroom and picked up comics and things of interest for them. Marvin and Stephen were our connection to the outside world. Stephen didn't want to go near the others for fear he would be next.

There was one especially difficult time when the Lord held us in His hands. Becky had come down with a high temperature and it continued to climb! I was very worried and had Becky in the bathtub with ice cubes in the water. She wasn't getting any better. Soon her temp was off the thermometer. The doctor told us to bring her to the clinic. I had already talked to Marvin and informed the doctor that we would take Becky to the hospital emergency room.

Various medical professionals were in and out of her cubical area. The decision was made to admit Becky into the hospital. The medical staff claimed it was scarlet fever as Becky's skin began to flake and peel off. This took several days to calm down. Marvin and I were assured that Becky would be okay, even though we— feeling very concerned—had to leave her in isolation for three days. Lots of friends prayed for her during those days of isolation; their support was greatly appreciated. What a huge sense of relief Marv and I felt when Becky was released and could come home! A great miracle!

In high school, Becky was very outgoing with a great smile and many friends. When she was a senior, she begged to have a Japanese gal, also a senior, live with us for a few months. (The length of her stay actually turned into eight months.) Marvin and I agreed and the arrangements for the visit were made. Hidako was a beautiful young woman. Upon her arrival she gave me a list of things she could eat. I told her, "Hmm, Hidako, while you are in America, you can learn about our foods and you get to eat what we Americans eat. You can make a Japanese meal for all of us whenever you care to do that." The thought of preparing food for ten people must have been overwhelming because she and Becky did make a meal—only once!

Both Hidako and Becky were interested in having great-looking hair. Hidako would brush her lovely, long black hair all of the time, all over the house. Consequently we caught the hair strands on our shoes or socks and the vacuum cleaner picked up the rest.

Becky also loved to work with hair, especially when baby-sitting the Stene girls. Her interest in styling hair actually bloomed into a career years later. Becky is now a professional hairstylist and owns her own hair salon. I am always very impressed with how talented she is as a stylist!

That summer when Hidako stayed with us, the teenagers from church went to Colorado on their youth trip, which gave her an opportunity to see more of the United States. Marv's nephew was also staying with us during those months. With five of our teenagers signed up, I gave up my car for the trip.

One day when my sewing machine was set up on the kitchen table, I had two quarters laying at the end of it. I left for a few minutes and then discovered that the quarters were gone. This was so upsetting because the family was being inundated with petty problems. No one confessed, so I "nailed" each one of the kids with the third degree and grounded all of them for the evening, which was a miserable time for all of us. When things quieted down, Greg (who was eleven years old) came to me crying and said he was so sorry. He had moved the quarters as an April Fools' Day prank. The quarters were scotch taped to the underside of the table. Why did it have to be my son?

Also at that time Jack and his new wife, Kay, managed to come about twice a year to visit her mother in Minneapolis, which made the trip to the Midwest more convenient and gave them a place to stay. Jack and Kay would pick up the boys and seemed to klutz through some visit time. Occasionally they sat and visited in the lounge of a special room at the airport and I tried not to make it any harder by questioning Greg, Doug, and Sean when they came back. Gifts were a different thing. Jack gave Greg and Doug big or good gifts and Sean a little thing. When the boys returned home, Sean would be crying because he wondered why his dad and stepmother didn't love him. At one point I called Jack to ask that they not bring any gifts if the presents couldn't be more evenly distributed in value. At least they made the effort to give presents.

During the summer when Greg was fourteen years old, he stayed with his dad and stepmother in Alaska and was able to travel with his dad to Norway for a conference. Doug was also invited to spend summers in Alaska at different times, and they made the same promise to Sean but never asked him to come.

Injuries sometimes happened to our active teenagers. Rodney enjoyed running, biking, and building things. As he worked on the construction of a huge glider, he had his young siblings and neighbor kids very excited about his project. Marv and I were not as serious. We were, however, quite surprised when we found out what Rod did to test it! He had convinced his friends to take him in the back of a pickup truck. One end of a rope was tied to the truck and the other end to the glider, which allowed him to fly as high as the rope would go. The driver stopped for the stop sign and Rod tangled with the electric lines and fell. The police came to the house with the news and we met Rod in the emergency room and saw bones in his arm protruding through the skin. Later, the glider was broken into pieces by Marv and burnt! (Rodney did, however, set a good example by being a studious student and he graduated with honors from high school. What a proud moment that was for Marv and me!)

There was also the time when the boys were playing football in the snow at Nelson's house with some of their seven children. Greg got tackled, bending his right femur the wrong way and causing it to snap. This required a very long cast on his very long leg for a very long time! We had to cut his trouser leg along the inside seam and safety pinned it together. The cast fought rough and hard on his bedsheets. The good news was that Greg's femur continued to grow taller. His miracle!

Years later, Greg is special in so many ways. It seems like I'm shrinking in height now but when I hug him or stand by him it feels so comfortable and good. He works hard and can do so many things. My father was a contractor. He and Greg had a very close relationship. If Dad were still living, he would be very proud of Greg. Greg has quick, no-nonsense answers and explanations for everything. He is also a great chef! He worked at a Mr. Steak restaurant and the restaurant at the downtown St. Paul airport during high school. For years I have never been allowed in his kitchen. He is a great father and grandfather.

Today, I am still learning from my family and the "grands" and the "great grands." I always love to hear about what they are doing, their travels, and what new opportunities have come up for them, and I keep them in my prayers.

Chapter 14

WONDERFUL TIMES AT OUR LAKE HOME

One time while Marvin, the kids, and I stayed at a rented lakeshore cabin, it rained continuously for three days and we became stir-crazy. On the third evening, Marv and I decided to change into our swimsuits and stepped out into the rain, using bars of soap to get clean. The kids thought this was great fun! Just try to picture nine of us goofing around in the evening rain with soap and giggles and chasing and sliding on the wet ground! Pure joy!

After that weekend, the idea of owning a getaway place was given serious thought! Marvin decided to take me to check out some mobile homes for sale. We bought an old, very used and faded, 10 ft. x 50 ft. mobile home. Marv had the trailer towed to Bone Lake in Wisconsin and parked on a lake lot at a resort.

This place of rest, relaxation, and fun times became known as the Lake Home. To make it possible for our family to fit in, trundle beds that looked like army style were used in one bedroom for the boys. The beds could be folded up and stored In a closet as needed so the boys could play inside on rainy days. Becky was given the smallest bedroom and Marvin and I used the third bedroom, which was closest to the kitchen. The old carpet was torn out and I scrubbed and waxed the floor to start the first year. This flooring worked well because it was easy to sweep the sand back out the door a couple of times each day!

The exterior of our trailer also needed some renovation. Marvin tarred the roof and the two of us painted the exterior walls white with red trim. My wonderful dad built a big deck with stairs (also painted red) off the living room/kitchen door.

Our dear friends, the Stene family, who lived across the street from our house, would come with their five young children. Curt helped us hang a rope swing from a great tall tree. On the rope was a board for the kids to sit on while swinging back and forth or twirling while getting dizzy twisting the rope in one direction and letting it spin back.

When I first met the Stene's, I felt very nervous. I knew I was up for inspection. Their youngest child liked me; he sat on my lap and played with my long string of beads. Darla was concerned that he would break them, but we did fine!

Whenever friends or relatives planned to come to the Lake Home, I always asked them to only bring some food to add to the meal so that I wouldn't be in the kitchen cooking all day. We sat around a long fold-up table for meals. My folks also gave us a metal round table with four metal chairs (also painted red!) that were used outside for serving food and playing tabletop games at anytime. Our trailer was situated across the drive and yard of an outhouse. This came in handy for our large gatherings of family and friends!

Our next purchase for the Lake Home was a large, old pontoon boat. My job was to clean and remove old paint and rust with Naval Gel and paint the pontoon with marine paint. In preparation for this work, Marvin backed the pontoon into our garage so that dirt and leaf debris wouldn't drift onto the wet paint and ruin it. The two garage windows and the big double door were kept open. Bright navy blue was his color of choice and I attacked the job with gusto! It didn't take long before I was ready to collapse just from inhaling the fumes! I was laid out on the grass in our backyard. I had to explain to our concerned kids what had happened. I couldn't move or breathe well! How could people sniff the likes of this odor to get high and become so sick? Obviously, the rest of the painting job was completed while the pontoon sat halfway out of the garage!

Our resort shore was weedy and unfit for swimming. Marv's solution for this was to transport the whole family out and about on the pontoon and anchor it in the middle of Bone Lake to let everyone swim. The three youngest children learned to swim wearing life jackets and getting pushed into the water by the older ones. Marvin mastered the operation of the boat motor while sitting in his new captain's chair and wearing his captain's hat because he wouldn't go into the water.

Friends and relatives were always welcome at the Lake Home and we really enjoyed spending time with them. Marvin and Curt Stene made up great goofy stories about our two families as native tribes and named them the Motleys and the Toolabys with a Princess Three Feathers. Those two storytellers kept us all laughing, at times even in tears! On the south end of Bone Lake was an island and that was where the Motleys and Toolabys "lived." We all looked forward to hearing those tall tales whenever the Stene family visited us. Darla and the kids would come and stay for a while without Curt in the summertime.

After a fun-filled weekend, we would return to Woodbury on Sunday evening. All of the dirty laundry was hauled to the basement and for me the process started all over again. I would wash and pack clothes for the coming weekend and take care of our needs at home for Monday morning and the coming week.

Those years flew by quickly. Enjoying this time away from the hectic pace of weekday activities and work was a real treat for all of us and continued until the older kids had to stay home for jobs, concerts, and parties. At that point, we started to make plans to sell the trailer and the pontoon. The rest of the family and I treasure many wonderful memories of the Lake Home.

Marvin and the teenagers having a fun time at
the Lake Home

Chapter 15

ROD & CLARICE SPEND TIME IN IOWA

*U*nbeknownst to us, the next fifteen months would be long and stressful, sprinkled with miracles from God and some good news! In the fall of 1974, Rodney, our son from Marv's first marriage, was enrolled as a freshman at Pillsbury Baptist Bible College in Owatonna, Minnesota and had joined the football team before classes started and the games began. During one of the football games held in mid-September, another player tackled Rodney really hard. After that injury, Rod suffered from headaches for a entire week. This didn't stop him from traveling with his roommate Gary and a few other students on a ministry outreach team the following weekend to Pilot Mound, Iowa. One of the youth events held that weekend was a hayride. Rodney played his trumpet and the young people laughed because his playing caused the cows to bellow and moo. After the hayride, food was served to the group. Rod filled up on hotdogs and became very sick, rolling his eyes and urping everything. Concerned about his friend, Gary told the pastor's wife that Rod had experienced headaches all week from a collision on the football field. It became evident that Rod needed medical care—STAT!

The local doctor was out of town so Rod was transported by ambulance to the hospital in Des Moines where the best neurologist in the region was attending patients. (This doctor would have been flown to Dallas to care for President Kennedy's injuries if he had lived a bit longer.) This was the beginning of a long year for Rod and our family. A tremendous miracle was coming.

At the Des Moines hospital, a medical team started to work on Rodney. After receiving the results of Rod's spinal tap, the staff had tried to locate us. Our son Greg was at home in St. Paul while the rest of us were in Moorhead with Mother Erickson. Greg got a call at home for the parents of Rodney. All he could tell them was that we were at Gramma Erickson's in Moorhead.

Well, there were a whole lot of Gramma Ericksons in that city directory. We didn't get a knock on the door from the police until 2 a.m. to ask if Rodney was our son. Yes! The police officer gave us the details of Rodney's hospitalization and the phone number to reach the doctor in Des Moines. We were told that a medical team was prepping for surgery while more tests were being run on Rodney. They asked if Marvin and I would each give our consent to surgery. (The medical staff would let us know when to come.)

I quickly prayed, "Oh, dear God, we are so helpless and you are in charge of this situation and we do pray for big miracles." I called the bus line, the airport, and the train station to find out if those schedules would work for Marv and me. Becky, a senior in high school, could drive the younger children home to St. Paul in her dad's car. None of those transportation options had a direct route to Des Moines. We started to pack and waited for the doctor's call before leaving. We decided to drop off the children at home in Woodbury where we'd pack some summer clothes for Marvin and me before rushing to Des Moines. I collected everyone's change so that we could stop and call the hospital from pay phones in route to Woodbury.

God provided Rodney with the best doctor of neurosurgery in the country and a qualified staff. The surgeon called us at Mother Erickson's house and talked to me first. I told him, "I'm Rodney's stepmother and I love him like my own. So, I give you my authority for surgery right now and here's his dad." I handed the phone receiver to Marvin, who was deeply distressed by the news. He told the doctor, "Yah, okay!" and handed the receiver back to me. The doctor then informed me, "You come now. I will do my best." Over the next few days, we learned he didn't usually offer families of his patients that kind of assurance. Other patients in the same condition as Rod hadn't been given much hope for survival. Yet this doctor gave me the direct number to the surgery room and said over the phone that he would do his best! After talking to the doctor, we ate a quick breakfast, called Greg to let him know our plans, and quickly departed.

That was the quietest ride our family ever had in a car. Each time anyone mentioned something that needed to be done, I put that person in charge of the task. I prayed fervently and tried to think of everything the kids would need to know. I realized that if God took Rodney home he would be with his dear mother and his heavenly Father. With certainty, I brought that up in the car. I felt it was important to cushion the news of a probable death in surgery before we saw Rodney again.

As we sped through towns, the children watched for pay phones. Each time Marv would stop the car as close as possible to the phone and we would hear the neurosurgeon telling the nurse who was holding the phone receiver that the surgery was going as planned and to call again.

After traveling for more than four hours across the state from Moorhead to St. Paul, we reached our home. When we walked into the house, there was Greg, a senior in high school, surrounded by some of our neighbors and a lot of friends from our church. He asked us what we knew. Our friends heard how grim and serious the situation really was for Rodney and assured us with their concern and offers of help. Sharon Peterson told us that she would organize meals for the kids. All of their support was definitely a RED carpet for us!

Marvin and I left as quickly as we could, reaching the huge hospital about 9 p.m. that evening. We were met with another precious RED carpet of support. The Lemans—the local Des Moines Baptist Church pastor and wife—planned to have us stay with them while Rod was hospitalized. The head football coach, Mr. Bob Eisman and his beautiful wife, Fritz; Terry, the assistant football coach; and Rod's roommate, Gary, who knew what Rodney had been through all week, were also there in the hospital waiting room along with the student outreach team from Pillsbury College, who were returning to campus.

What a loving heavenly Father I have! The Lord offered us emotional strength through these dear people. Both Marvin and I were exhausted from the trip and emotionally drained by the anxiety of not knowing what we would find. I knew that people were praying for Rod and his family and for his father Marvin to accept Christ as his Savior. A long chain of Christians petitioned the throne of grace, the King of Kings, for Rodney's physical recovery and to give us strength, comfort, and courage for such a time as this. The surgery had been completed before we arrived, so we did not see the doctor.

Shortly after arriving, Marvin and I really wanted to see Rodney, who was in postoperative care. We kept edging toward the Intensive Care Unit (ICU) door. One of the nurses stepped between the door and us to tell us what to expect. She wouldn't let us enter the room until we listened to her.

I still remember vividly how Rodney looked when we first saw him in the hospital bed. Wrapped on his head was a huge bandage. His neck and face were very, very red and VERY, VERY swollen, like no chin at all. His mouth was wide open—the beginning of not being able to take in liquids or foods by mouth—which caused a layer of crusty scabs to form inside it over time. Rod's wrists and ankles were carefully fixed to the bed rails because he had already gotten his thumbs under the bandage by his ears and tried to pull

each small improvement, I just thanked the Lord for His goodness for Rodney.

Every weekend college student teams from Pillsbury that had traveled to Iowa would stop to see Rod, sing in the hallway, and encourage Marvin and me. Occasionally, their singing bothered some patients or families of patients. When Rodney finally had his own hospital room, the students would go in to see him, even if he couldn't talk to them. Eventually, Marvin and I were told about the 24-hour prayer vigil the student body had set up. Individuals signed up for specific times to lift Rodney up in prayer until he recovered—students' miracle for us!

After each weekend at the hospital, Marvin drove back home on Sunday night to return to work during the week. We set two weekends for the whole bunch to be at the hospital and the medical staff let us take over a lounge. Having his siblings there was very good for Rod even if he couldn't talk or respond, except for squeezing a hand, which he did. He seemed to approve of our reactions and his siblings would get tickled and excited by it.

Get well cards arrived each day by the handfuls. When Rodney was moved into a room with two beds, the nurses let me cover two of the four walls with cards. As people walked by and took another look into the room, they usually commented. "WOW, he is popular!" I would always answer, "YES, he is surrounded by many prayer warriors."

One of the nurses we grew to love was Larry, a senior student, who was almost ready to graduate from nurses training. His care for Rod was so meaningful to us. As Rod watched, Larry would ask me a lot of questions about him and also about my faith. During lunch one day, a nurse came in with a little cup of pills. I was alarmed because Rodney still had IV's, a scabby mouth, and was only sucking small ice chips—definitely not ready for swallowing any size of pills. Larry was holding the pills when another nurse delivered a big meal. Larry set the pills down and started to feed Rodney. Feeling alarmed, I reacted, "Oh, please don't, Larry. Something is very wrong there. Rod's mouth and throat are still covered with scabs. Can we try Jello instead because it would feel so jiggly and sucking it should be great?" After I asked this, another nurse whisked the medications away while telling us that these didn't belong here. Soon the meal disappeared, too. Larry and I just looked at each other and I assured him this wasn't his fault. However, he needed to see it played out. Larry brought some gelatin dessert and Rod enjoyed it. Later that afternoon after his shift, Larry came back to visit us and he accepted Christ as his Savior. Another wonderful miracle!

During Rodney's stay in the hospital, a student from the college sent a lengthy get-well letter with a notice of all the demerits Rod had acquired by being absent, late for classes, not cleaning his room, failing to turn in papers, not going on outreach trips, not attending band rehearsals, not practicing football, having a shaved head, and so on. It was such an enormous list of demerits that we really laughed about it. Eventually we read it to Rod, and he just smirked! A miracle!

Marvin and I and the kids also had "angels." The Lemans welcomed us into their home and fed us many meals. Granella Leman taught me many wonderful things about hospitality, like setting the table ahead of time, so that your guests see they WILL get something to eat. Make sure to empty the bathroom wastebasket and slick up that room a bit because guests may have to use it and sit and look around while there. Carolyn was home a lot and she played the piano often, which was a soothing blessing to me. I used the city bus to travel to the hospital and learned how to catch it on time. Jan, another angel, who was Marv's first wife's cousin from Mason City, gave me their phone card for the long distance calls I needed to make. (Her husband Al worked for a phone company.) This was greatly appreciated because I could stay in touch with home, my folks, and my pastor.

A wonderful nurse who attended the Leman's church suggested that I stop in the gift store at the hospital and purchase an erasable tablet. Perhaps you remember this toy. A stylus was used to write messages on a sheet of plastic that covered the board. To erase the message, the plastic was lifted away from the board before writing again. What a great suggestion that was! That message board brought out of Rodney what he couldn't say yet. When Marvin left, he never said good-bye to Rod because we thought it was better if Rod did not connect Marv's coming and going with specific times. Using the tablet, I wrote, "Rod, we love you so much!" He grabbed it and scribbled, "Where Dad?" Before I answered him, I "flew" out to the nurses' station to show them the news and then hurried back to Rod. Then I called Marvin's boss to relay the message. I believed Marvin stood about 10 feet tall the rest of the day. From then on, I helped Rod compose short answers to questions and encouraged him to write until he felt tired.

Soon it was time for Rodney's girlfriend, Mary, to leave college for a break and return to her parent's home in Cottage Grove. Marvin brought her down to spend the weekend with Rodney. He was very excited to see her. The Friday night when Mary arrived, they let Marvin and I know that we should leave Rodney's room and sit in the lounge. Mary stayed in the hospital through the entire weekend to be close to Rod.

During that weekend, Mr. Bailey, an older gentleman, was Rodney's roommate. He really admired Rod, who had so many friends, a big family, many cards of support, and such "youthful strength." Mr. Bailey told me, "Your son has such strong arches." I didn't know that because I wasn't in the habit of checking the kids' arches! Mr. Bailey accepted Christ the first day Mary spent time with Rod. She meant business for the Lord. When Rod drifted off to sleep, Mary would visit and witness to Mr. Bailey, who was recovering from surgery. The previous Wednesday, Mr. Bailey had his gallbladder removed and was looking forward to Monday, because that was when the medical staff planned to remove the T-tube so he could be discharged and go home on Tuesday. Things didn't go as planned. Early Tuesday morning when I came in to visit Rod, I learned that Mr. Bailey had died and had gone to be with his Savior. Our daughter Becky contacted Mary's folks to let Mary know that the Lord had a job for her while she visited Rodney. What a miracle!

Rod spent three long months in the hospital and we saw a wonderful change in his health. Because of the health and cognitive gains he made, the medical staff allowed us to take Rodney home just before Christmas to find out how it would work to have doctors at the Minnesota University hospitals examine him.

Dr. Rammel, the Pillsbury College president, invited Marvin, Rodney, and me to come to Pillsbury College on the way back home and to appear before the student body. He also wanted us to visit with him privately. Dr. Rammel met with Marv and witnessed to him while the students were assembled. Rod, who sat in a wheelchair, and I were ushered onto the stage. I spoke to the students offering great thanks and praise and shared facts about many events that they could appreciate.

During the talk, I had to ask: "OK, which one of you sent the long list of Rod's demerits?" Everyone in the audience started to laugh! "How many of you prayed for him and us?" (Everybody responded.) They had taken up a collection for us, which came to more than $500. This was hard for me to believe and accept because this was a generous gift from students getting ready to go home for Christmas. "We are THANKFUL FOR ALL OF YOU and appreciated your visits and your singing from the extension teams." (I had notes and did say a lot more, but I can no longer remember it all.) Rod didn't say anything and wasn't ashamed of his shaved head and hair growing out. He did wave a lot when he saw someone he recognized. Their support was extremely uplifting for Rod and me!

When we finally arrived at home, his siblings were excited to see Rodney. I quickly looked for his trumpet and had one of the boys put it up in the attic crawl space before Rod could ask for it. But I didn't know that he still had his mouthpiece in his dresser drawer to blow into. The doctor told us that Rodney must be careful how he exerts himself—NO PRESSURE on his brain for a year! Marvin didn't discipline, so it seemed like I was treating Rodney like a little boy—oh yah, explaining to Rod how fortunate we were to have him alive and at home and getting well. "Yes, Rod, you can be well someday soon!"

One day Rodney filled the travel bags on his bicycle and buckled his sleeping bag on the back. He was all decked out to leave on a long bike trip. I kept an eye on him, even though I couldn't stop him. When he had been gone about twenty minutes, I called his dad who said I should contact the police. The officer told me that they had to wait twenty-four hours before searching for him. However, when I explained that Rodney had gone through three brain surgeries, had a soft spot on the right side of his head, and must exert "no pressure" on his brain, I learned that another officer had seen Rodney, thinking his shaved head might be because he had just returned from Vietnam—ah-hah! He knew where Rod was. The police officer headed out to apprehend him. Needless to say, Rod was really angry at me when he returned home!

How often in life we think that what we are doing is really helping others or counts for kudos when actually it is messing someone up. The frustrations that Rod felt were understandable and it pained me to watch him struggle as he worked toward becoming self-reliant! Rod had to learn everything over again—yes, everything! During that year, many times I asked God to give me strength and wisdom to cope with Rodney's disabilities and the ability to handle whatever lay ahead for me.

Today, Rodney looks great! He always seems to have a big smile and I enjoy visiting with him very much. I just wish it happened more often. Rodney attended Mankato State and met and married a great lady. He and his wife have been blessed with two very talented sons. The older son is the proud father of a very precious daughter.

Their younger son, Leif, has earned a bachelor's degree in industrial design at the University of Wisconsin-Stout. During his education, Leif designed many concept products for various industries, but one in particular really stands out because he showed me the project (called GenLink) and took my picture for it. That concept product was a device intended to bridge the technological gap between young and old.

Going into the project, Leif knew that many senior adults are technologically literate and engaging in social media, but he also knew there were many seniors without computer skills dealing with feelings of isolation and loneliness. These were the people he wanted to reach so he did his research by meeting with both seniors and caretakers to determine what the needs and opportunities were for such a product.

The concept product that began to emerge was a simplified computer system with a clean and simple touch-screen interface. It was not a full-featured computer but a portal to connect with loved ones from afar. Users could view images and content uploaded by friends and family to their GenLink device, removing the complexity of navigating a full-featured operating system and web browsers. Senior adults could also video chat and get the weather report.

After several years working as a professional industrial designer, Leif looked back on this project and told me that there are many things he would do differently now, but his passion for helping under-serviced people still exists. He looks forward to a career where he can make projects like GenLink become a reality. I am quite impressed with what Leif has accomplished and thank the Lord for blessing his parents, Rodney and Louise, in such a special way!

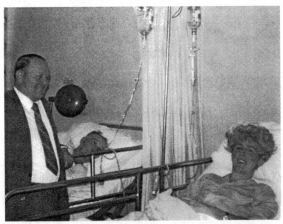

Pastor Ohmann, Mr. Bailey, and Rodney
who is wearing a wig

Chapter 16

"HOME FRONT LINE"

*W*hat Marvin and I didn't know or consider when we blended our two families together was the need for a place called "our" home. If it were possible to go back and make a change, I would definitely—and very seriously—recommend that we sell or move out of our two homes and purchase one that was new to all of us. My sons and I had moved a lot and Marvin's kids had lived in their house and neighborhood their whole lives. Marv and I had talked about giving this housing a year of testing. The year went by and we just continued the trial, erring through our lives without affording or thinking about a new place.

Adjusting to new situations as a family wasn't always dealt with when it should have been. We just went on. Perhaps we thought if we didn't discuss the issue, it would naturally be resolved. All of us had lost a lot of stability. Marvin's three sons and daughter were hurting and trying to deal with the loss of their mom. My sons were adjusting to their parents' divorce. I also didn't realize that God was there for us and wanted to comfort us. Many of my decisions were made by thinking that this is the way the situation is so deal with it even if it hurts for a while. Marv and I never knew what any one child was going through. Some days were loaded with raw emotions expressed by the kids, which was emotionally draining for me. Those feelings were hard for all of us to talk about. To prepare for what might happen, I would try to take a rest before the youngest one came home from school.

The "pecking order" in the house was established, stressed out, verbalized, fought for, and challenged often. One of the things I often answered the challenges with "just because I am the mother in our house."

The blending of Marv's and my family could have been much easier or lighter if we had a spiritual relationship with the Lord and repentant hearts. We didn't allow Him to run our lives and show His plans for us. What we did have was a lot of personalities, preferences, favorite foods, traditions, loyalties, generations of relatives, friends, and opinions. Someone in our family often seemed "unloved or rejected" and my new job was to love them all equally. My sister, Winnie, admonished me twice about losing my own boys while trying to love my new children equally.

After accepting Christ as my Savior, I wanted my family and my loved ones to know Him, too. I wanted to be a godly wife and mother to my family and felt very happy to have the Bible mean so much to me. I tried to grow in my faith walk with the Lord by listening to radio ministries and learning all that I could. Having a propensity to serve, love, and conquer for good was always going to halt MY ways and let God be first in all.

As the parent, one of my jobs was to transport the working teens to and from their jobs 'til they got their own transportation. During the drive time, I listened to the kid who was riding with me. Those conversations were important. So often at the supper table a lot was said, but there was always the one who wouldn't talk in front of everyone else.

It was quite fascinating to see what jobs our teenagers were hired for. Stephen worked in the mushroom factory and I had him leave his clothes in the garage, because they smelled so bad. (I'm allergic to mold.) Rodney worked in the huge, new Byerly's grocery store and he liked to bike whenever he could. I think his favorite assignment was the ice cream counter because he could remove the large "empties" or almost empty containers and eat any ice cream left in them when he got to the back rooms.

Our working teens had other jobs, too. Two of our teenagers worked for Green Giant and two worked at the Dorothy Ann Bakery and their skin broke out with blemishes. They would bring home the day-old goods, which the other family members loved. Greg worked for the railroad using a machine that raised the rails and gravel, replaced ties and cleaned the area, and then moved along. That job required an hour drive west from our home through both St. Paul and Minneapolis morning and night.

When I couldn't sleep, I would sit in the living room and pray for the teenager who was out way too late or it seemed like

God gave me a troubled heart for. When the teenager came in and found me waiting up, he would talk and ask me not to say anything until he was finished. Being "busted" was good for us, after which we would both sleep better.

I enjoyed preparing meals and baking foods and loved the company of guests who would eat with us. The few leftovers from a meal always walked away later that same night! I remember the time when my close friends, Jan and Dick, from New Richmond, needed some emotional support. Dick was a patient at Miller Hospital because of a large number of unidentified medical problems. Jan and their four-year-old Charie stayed with us. I taught Jan the easy way to drive to Miller, park there all day, and then return to our house in Woodbury. Jan listed off the very few things Charie would eat. For me, this was another "oh my" and a little miracle! That first evening I served a shrimp casserole and vegetables. There were ten of us at the table and Charie was sitting between two of the boys. One of them started to plop food on her plate and I said, "OH, no, she won't" and then just let it go. Charie learned to eat what was served to the people sitting around her at the table. Dick had mono, pneumonia, and a severe allergic reaction to penicillin and was in serious trouble for several days. He did recover and we all rejoiced. Big miracle for them!

For me, my biggest goal while raising our family was to learn that there was life after death and divorce. Some weeks were harder for me than others. One weekend night in particular I remember quite clearly. Marvin's mom was traveling on the late Saturday night bus from Moorhead to Minneapolis to visit us. It had been a busy day of housework and I still had to prepare for the Sunday meals. The plan was for Marvin to pick up his mom at the bus station. That evening, Marv had been drinking and wasn't able to walk to his car, nor drive! With my hair rolled up in big rollers, I tied a scarf around my head and took off in my car, not as happy as I should have been. The bus was late to arrive so I sat inside the bus station to watch for Mother Erickson. We didn't get home until 1:30 a.m. What a surprise we had when we walked in the back door! Oranges had been thrown all over the kitchen and family room. Those stuck on the ceiling dripped down, some laid smashed on the floor, and the juice ran down from those splattered on the walls. The whole place looked like an all-night sticky mess to clean up. I helped Mother Erickson walk through the room without slipping and helped her get settled for the night. I told her I was going to sleep on the couch and that later we would find out what happened.

When I woke up, I discovered the mess in the kitchen was gone. I never did find out who cleaned up the sticky, crushed oranges. Marv couldn't and his mother and I didn't, so I guess I will never know.

As to why there was a sticky mess in the kitchen, that was easier to figure out. When Marv and I got married, Becky had a pet cat that she was in charge of. One winter day when Becky came home from school, she found the cat frozen in the window well. A few years later, thinking if Becky had a cat, I told Greg he could have one if he took care of it. Marvin disliked that cat and was usually very mad at Greg or his cat—consequently the "orange crush"!

As our teenagers moved out and started down their own career paths, my responsibilities changed. Meals took less time to prepare. The chauffeuring of teenagers came to an end. They became very busy with their own lives as young adults.

Shortly before Greg graduated from high school, Marvin told him to get out. Greg lived in his car while finishing his senior year. After graduation he and his friend Brian traveled a bit, heading to Florida and then returning in the middle of July. When I opened the drapes in the living room on the morning of July 17th, I saw his car with condensation on the windows parked out in front. That day, it was my birthday. Later he came in to give me a hug and visited with me. What a great birthday present that was! Best miracle!

Marvin also told Douglas to get out of our house. Doug headed to Anchorage, Alaska and lived with his dad and his stepmother Kay. Later, he moved to Sri Lanka—the Pearl of the Indian Ocean and also the longest democracy in Southeast Asia and predominantly Buddhist. Sri Lanka had significant importance during the time of "The Silk Road" and has one of the longest documented histories of over 3,000 years. Doug spent six months traveling on foot (with a huge pack or "whatever" supplies he needed) to other parts of eastern countries. Riding on top of a train would not be my choice of transportation! Doug learned a lot about coffee, tea, sugar, rubber, cinnamon, mining, and the

British Colony. While he traveled, he only sent two postcards. I was never certain that I would see him again.

Upon returning from Southeast Asia, Doug resided in Homer, Alaska and eventually was hired to work on the Indonesian "mother" ship for freezing and canning fish, located outside the twelve mile zone along Alaska's shoreline. Doug inspected each haul of fish that was brought onto the ship and then priced it for the owner. I asked Doug if this work was rather dangerous when they thought his price was far too low. He explained that he carried a knife and a gun. Only foreigners worked on the ship and little English was spoken so he did lots of reading. Doug told me about the day when he got into his wet suit and swam around the huge ship. As he swam, the foreigners followed him on deck, chattering and probably questioning his sanity in doing that.

Doug eventually knew if he ever wanted to marry it wouldn't happen while he worked that job on the ocean. Thus, he made some employment changes and returned to Homer. Later, after Marv died, Doug met Tessie, the love of his life. My mom, Sean, and I flew up for their wedding in Alaska. It was so great to see Doug, meet Tessie and her family, and be there on their special day. Tessie is one of twenty-four children and one of two sets of twins. Today, she is very precious to me.

While Marvin and I lived in Woodbury, we spent time redecorating our house to make it more comfortable for the whole family and a place of "nesting" for us. Marv and I both loved antiques and looked forward to Saturday mornings when the two of us went out for breakfast and then shopped at favorite antiques stores. These were perfect dates—alone for several hours and no drinking! I also loved shopping at garage sales and refinishing wood and upholstering some of the pieces I purchased. These pieces were displayed with some of Marv's inherited, wooden treasures.

In preparation for one Christmas, with the boys scattered away from home, Marvin and I moved into the long room (boys' old bedroom) and I used our former bedroom to work on old trunks, one for each of them as a gift. I searched for seven old trunks that I could restore and stripped them on the brink of our driveway. This couldn't be a surprise for lack of hiding room! One day, Greg stopped in and asked what I was doing. I explained and said, "This one will be yours!"

He shot back, "Well, I don't want an old trunk!"

"Oh boy! What if they all feel like this?" I thought. I kept going with the restoration. When the weather got colder, the work had to be done in our old bedroom, which was ventilated by opening the windows as needed. Eventually when a trunk was finished, it was displayed with other antiques. Guess what? On Christmas day, Greg was the first to ask Marv if he could use the van to take his trunk home. Hmm, nice miracle!

What a pleasure it has been watching my family grow with the addition of spouses and seeing what fine people they are. Stephen was the first son to get married. His wife, Jeanna, wore his mom's wedding dress and her young daughter was the flower girl. Rodney and Louise were next to wed, followed by Greg and his first wife, and then Rebecca and John. Douglas and Tessie were married in Homer, Alaska, and traveled to Minnesota so she could visit the Minnesota State Fair. Paul and Elizabeth got married after Douglas. The last of the immediate family weddings was when Greg remarried after his divorce. He married Monica.

Through the years, the Lord has blessed me in so many ways, especially with these adorable and talented grandchildren: Ryan, Zarah, Hillary, Ed, Ella, Heather, Waylon, Jodi, John, Jon, Bjorn, Jessie, Lief, Mandy, Sam, and Ian. Some of my grandchildren are now busy raising their own families. My precious great grandchildren are Cyrena, Malachi, Jocelyn, Anya, Lillia, Isabella, Dynamite, and Askel.

Greg and Monica Doyle along with Doyle and
Erickson family members in 1994

Jodi, the first party girl in Clare's shop, with her parents and brother

Paul holding Bachelor of Arts diploma received at University of Minnesota, Morris— June 1984, Happy Day!

Dick and Jan—special friends!

Chapter 17

"ANTIE CLARE'S" FIRST & SECOND DOLL HOSPITALS

s the boys moved out and left the basement rooms, Marvin removed the bunks and a wall making a larger open space. I used this opportunity to start a doll hospital in a small area of the basement. My doll club was the first group to hold a meeting there to check it all out. Our back yard was also small but private and worked well for wonderful picnics and doll-club friends to sit and visit. Mom also collected dolls for years and would travel with me to meetings once a month. This allowed me to spend a special day with her.

I had become "Antie Clare" to my relatives and later to my neighborhood, so the new name for my business became "Antie Clare's" Doll Hospital, Shop & Museum. Over the years, plans for a doll shop and museum swirled in my head and I stashed many notes in the glove compartment of our car about having a doll shop and museum.

My personal collection started with my childhood dolls and grew in number, taking over an entire wall in the long bedroom, which became Marv's and mine. In the chapter on my childhood, I told about playing with Karen. Her dolls were wonderful and baby sized. When Karen left her Effanbee doll with caracul hair and badly torn cloth shoulders leaning against the garbage can in their garage, she said I could have it, so I took it home. The doll was wearing a beautiful pink coat and cap that her grandmother, "Mor-Mor" had sewed. My mom repaired the doll's shoulders and "WE" walked the doll back to Karen's house. I apologized to them. Karen and her mom gave me the doll and kept the coat and cap. This doll actually was the beginning of my museum and Victorian birthday parties for "little ladies."

My granddaughter, Jodi, was the first party girl in my doll shop and museum! (Jodi had been staying with Marv and me until her mom felt better because she had been quite sick. Her mom had requested that we give Jodi a great birthday party, so we did!) For the party, Jodi wore a bridal veil and her six friends brought their dolls and wore my gloves. Those adorable young girls sat at two little tables while I served them tiny foods like Cheerios, chocolate chips, marshmallows, candy, etc., and, of course, a small cake that had a doll figurine on it. The girls played sitting games like searching for something in the room. Jodi opened her gifts and after about two hours the girls went home.

One day, my folks came to meet with me before they left on a short trip. They shared some good news: upon their return, I would be receiving about 700 of Mom's dolls for the museum. (Mom owned a huge collection of dolls!) With that donation, my business needed a larger space so I leased the south end of the clock shop building on White Bear Avenue in St. Paul. What a blessing that was! We retrofitted the store with my brother Butch's carpenter skills and Winnie, Edna, and other gals' talents were used to design and make snazzy girl things. The large cabinets from my home doll hospital were moved into the shop and I set the business in motion.

At first, we hosted one party for eight young girls on a Saturday. Later, at my largest shop, the business grew to five (two hours) little girl parties on Saturdays. I bought the "sweets" and we added a collection of hats to match the gloves. I also hired two high school girls dressed like Barbie dolls to be the party hostesses. The girls didn't like wearing the outfits and a matching big bow in their hair, but their pictures went all over the world as the birthday party hostesses! The girls either became great at handling their roles or they quit.

The party festivities also included a tour of the doll museum—for which I made up stories to go with the Erickson manor scenes—and there were a few sitting or searching quiet games for the young girls to play. Except for Marvin, the whole family was depicted in the Erickson Manor, along with some relatives and my favorite Edna.

One of my stories featured a doll named "Aunt Agatha." She was named for a snooty aunt from the cities. The young girls were told how Aunt Agatha was sitting in the dining area waiting for Clare to visit her and her two daughters. (That doll had her legs crossed and was swinging one, which showed her ankles—a no-no during Victorian times. A small visible mouse was also displayed under her skirt.) Aunt Agatha had a hissy fit when she found out about the mouse. (The guide or hostess showed the girls what a hissy fit was and they would all squeal and scream loudly. Everyone in the building knew immediately what was being shown on the tour at that time.)

Other scenarios I created in the museum included "Paul" standing in the kitchen while the "maid" was baking cookies. He was devouring a handful while she was "rubbering" on the phone. Two of his "friends" were playing checkers on the floor. Wet mittens were drying toward the back of the iron stove. Two "young girls" were playing dress up in the "attic"—one being "Kay," my childhood friend—and were oblivious to the weather or time. The dog ended up with the young girls and, of course, there were cobwebs and spiders and even a mouse or two in that attic. (All of the clothes on those two dolls were too large for them as if they were pretending to be big ladies.)

During all of my trips to antiques shops or gift shops I would use my eye antennas to search for miniatures to include in scenes. It became a delightful challenge to find pieces in different sizes to embellish the displays and very gratifying for me to watch my customers admire the dolls in the scenes.

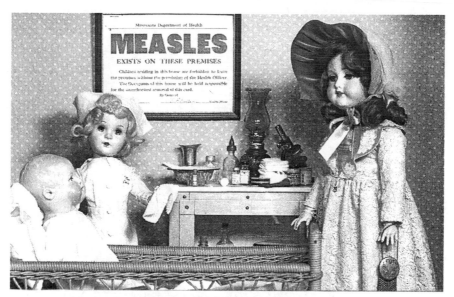

One of the scenes in Clare's doll museum

Marvin and Clare on their last short trip

Chapter 18

MY "ENGLISH EMILY" AND THE NORTH SHORE

pending time with Emily and at the North Shore along Lake Superior was a very special part of my life. Emily, a dear elderly lady, came often into my doll shop with her friend and would talk to me as she looked over her eyeglasses. I soon called that her "grandmother look" and an English one at that. Emily immigrated to the United States as a young girl and had to take care of her siblings. Times were tough for her family; they didn't have much. She shared stories about coming through Ellis Island and loved to tell me about her family's history.

While visiting my shop one day, Emily asked if my husband and I would like to come up to her cabin sometime. I responded with "hmm," thinking that Marvin wouldn't really enjoy staying at an elderly lady's cabin. As a result, I forgot to ask Marvin about it. The next time she stopped in the doll shop, Marvin was also there. She asked if he was my husband, so I introduced them and got busy with a project again. That night Marvin asked me when I had planned to tell him that we had been invited to her lake home. I told him that I was sorry for not mentioning it and that I didn't know where the cabin was located. Well, he knew! The cabin was twenty-two miles from the Canadian border on Lake Superior!

After that first visit, Marv and I stayed at Emily's cabin many times through the years when her family wasn't using it. We would pick Emily up on a Friday right after work and travel up there for the weekend. At first she just stayed there until her family came and brought her back with them. I usually was exhausted from the work at the shop and would sleep late on Saturday morning because the fresh air, the smell of pine trees, and the ambiance of the water slapping against the rocks were enough to hypnotize me.

What a great vacation we always had with Emily! The three of us especially enjoyed eating at Betty's Pies in Two Harbors, having High Tea, or enjoying the Sunday brunch at the beautiful and historic Naniboujou Lodge, near Grand Marias. We also kept meals simple so as not to work all the time.

When I was younger, I would weed her English garden while staying there. However, over the years the garden got smaller and smaller. Many people loved to see her flowers and the elves in the garden and would start taking the whole plants—beautiful red poppies and the different colored lupins. Now those flowers bloom up and down Highway 61 along the North Shore!

Emily and I had many wonderful conversations. She would tell me about the good times and the sad times that happened in her life, like the following story. One day Nick (her husband), Emily, and a lady friend were on the Gunflint Trail picking berries. Emily told me that her friend had started to feel sick so she asked Nick to finish picking berries quickly so they could return to the cabin. Twenty minutes later, Emily and her friend started to call Nick and look for him, but he was nowhere to be found! The side of the road where they had been picking berries was all low bushes, compared to the wooded area with tall pine trees and no berry bushes across the road. The ladies hailed a vehicle coming south and told the driver Emily's husband was missing. Eventually, the police arrived and search parties were formed.

Emily also told me how volunteers went out daily for weeks to search for Nick with no success. Each day she met with the search party and told the volunteers about Nick and provided a clothing article for the dogs to catch his scent. Emily also shared about Nick's faith and character with the volunteers. In order to see each other, one young couple, whose parents disapproved of their dating, became volunteers and searched together. The young man came to Emily one morning and asked about Nick's faith because he wanted to be like the man he had been hearing about.

Nick never was found. When I learned about her husband's disappearance, I asked Emily how she could turn all of this over to God. She explained that she had petitioned God for a good sign and because of this prayer she had witnessed that young man asking to be born again. Emily also had invited both sets of parents to come to her place and encouraged them to allow these two special, young adults to date and possibly marry, which the couple later did.

As a hobby, Emily started to paint porcelain tiles for her fireplace. Each tile featured Minnesota flowers or berries. Her artwork even made the local news, bringing a lot of people and many friends to see her fireplace. Whenever I stayed at the cabin, Emily always had that special couple's photo of their family displayed on the mantle.

Emily was a beautiful woman of God for all of us to emulate. Her kindness and generosity was extended to many "neighbors." Through Emily, I was blessed with many new friends up and down the North Shore. She and I would also drive up to Portage for the senior lunches and enjoyed visiting with more neighbors while there.

Years later as her health declined and after Marvin had died, Emily needed someone to stay with her at night. I volunteered to spend that time with her and left for work from her house. Her guys moved a single bed into the dining room for me to sleep on. We did okay with this arrangement.

After that, Emily needed to reside in a nursing home and I would be her private guest for dinner in a small solarium once a week. At one point because of her failing health, she was admitted to a downtown hospital. I remember one evening when I had buzzed into her room to see her—oops—visiting hours were just over. I saw her gagging but no medical staff was around! The nurse's call button was not within her reach. I rushed to turn Emily on her side and elevated the head of the bed. For years, Emily had been stooped over, so she would not have been able to breathe flat on her back. That night, I stayed in her room until 2:30 a.m. and kept removing the phlegm from Emily's mouth until she could breathe easily. Not one nurse or person came by or stepped into her room while I cared for her. That made me think that the medical staff could easily have told Emily's family the next day that she had died in her sleep. Ooooh! From then on, Emily named me her angel.

For me, Emily was an unbelievably special woman, whom I will always admire. She shared her life, her family, her friends, and her cabin on Lake Superior, her home and meals in St. Paul, and her stories about family and life in England and in St. Paul with me. How blessed I was to know her!

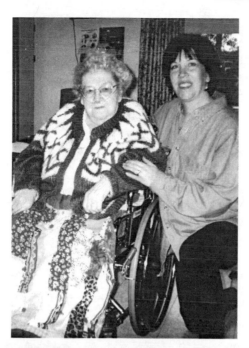

Emily and her
granddaughter
Maria

Clare with Emily's "great grands"–wonderful little girls!

Chapter 19

UNEXPECTED & UNPLANNED

Our friends, Harry and Marlette, and Marvin and I took short trips around Lacrosse, and east to the Frank Lloyd Wright House, New Lisbon, House on the Rock, and Baraboo, Wisconsin. A great place for us to eat was at a Perkins Restaurant because of the variety on the menu. While dining, we noticed that Marvin was not finishing his meal. He had lost a lot of weight and wasn't eating much.

On those trips, as we walked around, Marvin would often come up behind me quietly and walk "in-tune" with me for as long as possible. Eventually people would look or laugh or say something that let me catch on. This was a delightful thing for him to do, but it embarrassed me!

Marvin wasn't drinking or smoking on these get-away trips and seemed more content. In fact he was the driver and that always made him feel happier. These trips with friends were our last, enjoyable times together before circumstances changed.

Upon returning home, Marvin slid back into his old habits and acted ornery and seemed quite ill. Concerned about him, I called my Christian doctor. Dr. Rupp said to come in at 8 a.m. Monday morning and he would examine Marvin. I was praising God for this doctor and calling the prayer chain, Marvin's mom and boss, my folks, and all our kids, asking them to pray for Marv because I planned to tell him about the appointment on Monday. "Mar-va-sooovious" is what I heard when I told him the plan. Yes, he was VERY angry with me. He hated doctors and nurses because his first wife died under their care. His boss was, however, pleased with this news and told me about some of the problems the staff had experienced with Marv's customers. Elmer, a co-worker, was also glad that Marvin was seeing a doctor.

Marvin drove his new red truck and I followed him to the clinic. As he headed into the building, he wouldn't talk to me. When Marv came out of the clinic, he was still very angry. Marvin returned to work and I went to my doll hospital/shop and got busy with projects and customers until Dr. Rupp called me. He told me to bring Marvin to Bethesda Hospital for more tests as soon as possible. "Why?" I asked. After quizzing him, he finally said, "Clare, Marvin has massive cancer tumors of the esophagus and we need to be able to run more tests. I have them ordered to be done as soon as you can get him there."

After hanging up, I prayed. "Oh, God, we really need you now. Marvin doesn't know you personally and he is not ready to die. Oh, dear God, speak through me. I'm yours."

Shaken by this news, I called Rollie. Without mentioning cancer, I explained that Marvin needed to come home and go to the hospital as soon as possible for more tests. Rollie called Marv on the truck radio, but he ignored it. In the meantime, I talked to my staff and then hurried home to pack his suitcase, write notes to the kids, and wait and wait. Finally, Marv's Wards van came up the driveway with his Christian friend, Elmer, driving him in it—for the last time. This was our first of many RED CARPETS! My eyes and my heart were crying for Marv, but I needed to be calm and strong and honest as we sat on the side of the bed and discussed what I had been told. He knew that I did not lie, cheat, or steal and that I loved him with all of my heart. This was a warm and tender moment of assurance—the calm before the storm in a way.

As we entered the hospital room, I read the HOSPICE sign posted beside the door and let out, "Oh, you, lucky duck, you get a single room!" That was 1984 and the concept of hospice care was still new to us. The staff was there to help Marvin get settled in the room, administer more scans and X-rays, and offer him a liquid supper. Afterwards, Dr. Rupp came and sat on the side of the bed, talked about the test results, and wrapped his arm around Marvin and prayed for us. What a grand opening to the next phase of our lives!

The next morning, the staff worked out plans for his diet; for surgery, treatment, and therapy; and to have our kids come in for a family conference on Wednesday evening to meet with the doctors and some staff. I also called my staff and folks, Marv's boss, and the prayer chains to ask them to support us with thoughts and prayers.

That afternoon Elmer called and asked if he could bring his youth pastor, Darrell, to talk to Marv about salvation. I knew how much Marv would hate that, but I asked him nicely and he agreed, "I guess so." I was thinking, "Oh, oh, WOW!"

When Elmer and Darrell came on Wednesday evening, they met with Marv in his room while the family meeting was being held. Becky was very upset that her dad wasn't at the meeting. I tried to reassure Becky that her dad had heard all of this for several days. I talked about how her dad would be in surgery the next morning and that it was important for Marv to hear about salvation again. When the three men came to the elevator near the meeting lounge, oh dear, I could tell that nothing had changed.

We were all together as a family sitting in the hospital lounge, meeting with the oncology and surgical staffs to learn about Marvin's cancer tumors that had taken over his esophagus. At the same time, Pastor Bruce was leading a special prayer meeting at the St. Anthony Village Hall, where Ambassador Baptist held services. Teens and adults joined in corporate prayer before the throne of God to petition for Marvin's salvation. That wonderful miracle came later that evening!

Chapter 20

MARVIN HAS A CHANGE OF LIFE

Around 9:30 p.m., everyone departed after the family meeting in the hospital lounge. Marvin and I started to walk down the quiet, dimly lit corridor to his room. (In the oncology wing, many of the patients were probably experiencing pain or not sleeping well.) Marv grabbed my upper arm where it was soft and flabby and made it wiggle and tease me. Then, he started to slip and fall next to me! I wanted to scream . . . "Ooouch!" I looked confused as if to say, "What is this about?" I didn't want to fall on Marv and make his condition even worse. Marv kept pinching my arm until he regained his balance. Then while still standing in the hallway, he told me, "I want you to give me Roman's Road once more!"

"Oooh! Really? I can't remember it now!" Even though I had shared it with people many times, I was stunned and couldn't recall it right then.

Marv—very calmly—said, "Help me get into the bed and then show me in your Bible."

"OH! YES! SURE!"

When we walked into his room, the nurse was slicking his bed and had prepared the bed for him to recline almost upright. Fluids surrounded his heart, making it impossible for him to lie down and breathe. Marvin could only sit up to sleep. I told her, "Marvin is going to accept Christ as his Savior now and this is the most important thing in his life to do." Well, she left in a big hurry, leaving the door open. While I was sharing scripture with Marv, the nurse shuffled papers just outside the door. It will be a joy to meet that gal in heaven one day and see if she too made that decision. Oh how wonderful it was to hear Marv repent and ask Jesus to come into his life. After praying, Marv grabbed my head and hugged it. My nose was somewhere on the Roman's Road in my Bible and my glasses were bent when Rodney walked into the room. Precious miracle!

Rod asked with a puzzled voice, "Dad, what are you doing to Clarice?" and came over to pull us apart until Marv replied, "Rod, I needed to get saved tonight!" What pure joy! Rod hugged both of us. That felt so good. We all had big smiles!

Then, Marv wanted to call our friends, Harry and Marlette. He told Marlette that the doctors and nurses could clean him up AND out, but he needed to have Jesus clean up his heart! While Marv talked on the phone, we heard KTIS radio station playing the song, "Shackled by a heavy burden, 'neath a load of guilt and sin, Then the hand of Jesus touched me, And now I am no longer the same." (Lyrics by William J. Gaither) He told Marlette he could hear her stereo and they were playing his song! "This is MY song now!" Marvin said. Marlette hurried upstairs to tell Harry the wonderful news. He went to bed early every evening because he always got up at 4 a.m. to go to work, but that night he was happy to be awakened. For fifteen years we had prayed for this! Praise be to God!

I had no idea that Rod had stayed after the family meeting to jog outside around the hospital building and would have just gone home without him. I needed to calm down and pray about the early morning surgery. I didn't know whether the surgery would be the long version and the surgeon would remove the cancer and hook the stomach up to the top of the esophagus or the shorter version (the cancer couldn't be removed) for inserting a tube so that Marv could take in liquid nourishment right into his stomach.

When Rod and I finally arrived at home, the house was quiet. I shared the good news about how Marv "found" Jesus by calling our pastor and close friends who were prayer partners, and then I headed to bed, leaving it all in the Lord's hands.

Early the next morning, I headed back to the hospital and waited to hear the outcome. Marv's surgery was the shorter version. The medical team found him full of cancer. From then on Marvin could only have ice chips and about two cups of Ensure a day via the gastrectomy. The doctors gave him six to eight months to live. (Marv actually had less than four months and his 57th birthday to celebrate.) Our daughter-in-law, Jeanna, found and cut out a headline in the Sunday paper that said, "MARVIN

HAS A CHANGE OF LIFE" and tacked it to the bulletin board above his bed.

Between radiation treatments, chemotherapies, and more stays in the hospital, Pastor Bruce held many Bible studies with Marvin and a friend named Jerry. This was really like helping both Marvin and Jerry walk to the Kingdom! Pastor asked if I would be a prayer partner and stay out in the family room. (This way I wouldn't get involved, either.) Both men pelted Pastor with questions and what a blessed time this was for them.

The doctors wanted Marvin to have radiation and chemo to calm his organs down and do as much good as possible. Those days were very hard for Marv as he dealt with pain and agony.

The name of my business, "Antie Clare's" Doll Hospital, Shop & Museum, and the address and phone number were painted on the back of my car. Because of this advertisement and as owner of the business, I wore dresses and made certain I was presentable every day. For therapy appointments, we parked in a small lot reserved for radiation patients, and, of course, when others came into the waiting room, they looked around to see who might be "Antie Clare."

One day when Marv and I returned home after one of his treatments and I had just helped him get settled, Greg walked into the house and asked, "Where are you going?"

"We just got home from Marvin's therapy," I replied.

"Why are you all dressed up?"

"Because I want to represent my business and my testimony and besides I'm your mother and I have an image to uphold."

"Oh, image, schmimage, you're my mother! Well, could Marv stand a ride to Minneapolis for about an hour and a half?" Greg asked.

"Oh, YES! I think he would love it because none of his kids have been with him or called for almost two weeks. He is quite hurt by that."

Greg asked Marv to come for a ride, which took him out of the confinement of the house and his daily routine. They had a good trip.

One thing I observed while accompanying Marv to appointments was that patients waiting for radiation and chemo treatments looked pretty sad! The male patient scheduled ahead of Marv each day signed in one time as "Robert Redford." When the nurse called that name, I exclaimed, "Oh! Robert Redford, I would like your autograph because my family won't believe I saw you today!" He was embarrassed and said I'd have to wait until he was finished with the treatment.

In visiting with his wife, I learned that they were meeting their three daughters for lunch and purchasing a wig for him because he would loose his hair soon. We didn't have to do that! Marvin had what I called his halo around his head above his ears. Sure enough one morning his halo was on his pillow.

The hospital staff seemed to keep the same room open for Marvin whenever he was in and out with his complications.

During one hospital stay, the chaplain stopped in and asked how Mr. Erickson was. Marv wouldn't talk to him, so I said, "The doctors tell us he has terminal cancer and we do not have wills made out. Could you help us?" After explaining this, the chaplain took his coat off and left the room to get the phone number of a lawyer in our county. Marvin ignored important topics that should have been seriously researched. What a relief that was for me when the chaplain returned with a phone number.

I contacted the attorney referred and made arrangements. During the meeting, Marvin was smiling and pleased to see that the attorney was young and looked like John Denver, even his eyeglasses were similar. Marvin loved John Denver music. Within a couple of days, the attorney had drawn up a personal will for Marv and a business one for me. Marv was at home for the afternoon when the attorney brought the papers so I asked a neighbor friend and my sister Winnie to be witnesses for the signing of the documents. Prior to meeting with the attorney, Marv couldn't discuss this topic. He also never would talk about what he wanted for his funeral.

I spent time in the hospital lounge. When Marvin would join me, we met a nine-year-old angel! Her mom, who was staying just two rooms away from Marv's, was dying so the young girl came to see me in the lounge often over a few days. They were all born again. Her brother asked her to find a certain verse in the Bible. I was eating an apple, so I asked if she would like an apple party.

She agreed and after getting her an apple, we shared many good verses from the Bible for her mom.

She printed this message on my napkin (which I kept):

I have gone to prepare a place for you.
I will come again soon—
JESUS

That night I stopped at my shop and wrapped a small pair of bisque dolls for her. The next morning when I brought them to the hospital, I learned that her mom's room was empty and had been cleaned. I asked the nurse if I may have the address to send the dolls to her. And then, after some hesitation, the nurse decided to mail the package instead of sharing the address.

My staff made it possible for me to stay with Marvin almost all day and night at home or in the hospital. I did call in daily to talk with the staff. If I had been staying with Marv at the hospital late in the evening, I would stop in the shop at 2 or 3 a.m. just to see if there were things I could accomplish and tweak for the staff.

Marvin requested body massages all the time and I kept lotion nearby to ease some of his stress. I would talk about the memories—the things we made or did together. Marv would not kiss me—at first this really hurt my feelings—even though I reminded him that his cancer wasn't contagious! Instead God gave me these quiet times to choose to love him all over again and to confirm my love for him more and more. We had just walked through a difficult year of loveless days and lonely nights and for Marv so much drinking and smoking and a weight loss of 100 pounds. Perhaps, at that time he knew something terrible was going on in his body and refused to deal with his health.

During one appointment, the doctor asked Marv if he smoked and if he drank. Nothing more had to be said. Alcohol ruined so many beautiful times in our marriage and left so many hurts and scars—broken bonds of friendship and many missed pleasures. Words had been said that could not be taken back.

What a mighty God we serve! Marv told me, "I wish I had been a better father!" And, at another time he commented, "I'm sorry I didn't love you more."

As Marvin grew weaker, I asked Mother Erickson to come and be with us. On May 3rd of 1984, we borrowed a wheelchair so that I could get Mother Erickson in and out of the hospital without her having to walk. I also invited her three brothers and their wives to meet us in the cafeteria for the evening meal to see Marvin and his mom. Greg offered to bring Marv by wheelchair to the cafeteria while I brought his mom there. It was good for everyone to be together for a brief visit; even though it was not a celebration. Marvin's uncles and aunts and his mother all got to see him and say what was on their hearts before Marvin needed to return to his room.

The day had been long and packed. I was exhausted when I brought Marv's mom back to our home later that night. Sleep took me and I slept until the phone rang at 2:10 a.m. (May 4th,

1984). The nurse told me that Marvin had died and that I should to come to his room in the hospital. She also said she would call Dr. Rupp and tell him to meet me there. I suggested that it wasn't necessary to wake up Dr Rupp because he would be needed for surgery in a few hours. We all knew the cause of death, and yet I should have thought to say they could perform an autopsy if they would like to know the extent of his cancer.

The phone call alerted Mother Erickson, so I talked to her about waiting to tell the family until I came back in the morning and encouraged her to stay in bed and rest even if she couldn't fall back to sleep. I called Pastor Bruce and we met at Marvin's favorite Embers restaurant and planned his funeral. I did not know that Pastor Bruce had actually spent the previous evening in his office working on his plans for Marv's homecoming service. We found it all just went together smoothly. Just the day before, not knowing God's exact plans, I left Marv's room for a walk in the afternoon. From another part of the hospital, I phoned the local mortuary to ask what should be done when Marv dies. The directions were to pick up the phone during any hour of the day and give them the pertinent information. These were gentlemen I met through the White Bear Avenue Business Association.

After I arrived at the nurse's station and was ushered into the room, I saw Marvin's body lying flat, alone, clean, and neat. The darkened room made everything feel calm as if Marv was asleep, which told me the staff had moved his roommate elsewhere. I talked "at" him as I held his cold hand and praised the Lord with thanks for Marv's salvation. How special it was to know God had just ushered Marv into heaven! Sweet peace! What a Savior! "Marvin, I know you wouldn't want to come back and I'm so glad I learned to love you all over again with no strings attached. I look forward to seeing you in Glory soon." Tears streamed down my face as I thought about the truth of Marv's salvation being so close to his home going, the reality of God's presence in that room, and His wonderful gift of eternal life! I voiced my "love memories" and so many things we had done together. I had already promised Marv that I would do my best to love and guide all of our children as their mother, providing they would let me do this.

While still holding Marv's hand, I thought about so many events that had taken place in our lives. Marvin and I had been married for seventeen years. That was longer than his first marriage. I came into Marv's children's lives when they were deeply affected by their mother's death—grieving the loss of her—and weren't pleased to have her replaced.

Yet God loves us so much that He keeps all of our tears! To think He hears each one fall! I am definitely alone now but comforted by the sweet presence of the Lord.

Vernon May took this photo of Clare and
Marvin after church one Sunday.

The Erickson/Doyle family after Marvin's funeral

Chapter 21

BIG BUMP IN OUR BLENDED FAMILY

Thinking about "blended" families and how it has been more than 30 years since Marvin died, I'm ashamed to say that we still have challenges, walls, and broken bonding in our family. A blended family has a lot to learn and experience. It doesn't mean justice for all! My blender says: MIX, WHIP, BEAT, CHOP, PUREE, LIQUID and that could mean "creamed" in a family of our size.

Vern May, a photographer in my church, asked Marv and I to stay after the service on one particular Sunday to have our picture taken. This photo was special for Marv and me because it was the last one taken of us together.

Vernon offered his services again by asking me to gather the family on the following Sunday after Marv's funeral for a professional photo. I asked the whole family if they would like to attend the Sunday church service held at St. Anthony Village Hall and then afterwards allow Vern to take our family picture on the stage. Another red carpet for us!

My oldest daughter-in-law was most upset to think they had to attend that church service. I responded, "Vern is doing this for us and you don't have to come at all if you are going to be angry about coming." The picture was taken of the entire family. When looking at the proofs, we discovered Marv's mother had her eyes closed in the pictures and she had beautiful blue eyes! "No problem!" Vern told me. "We can give her blue eyes." Amazing!

In Marvin's will, he left everything to me. This included the family treasures, his guns, his newly acquired (and unpaid for) Dodge Ram truck, a big boat with motor and trailer, a nice big table saw, an electric organ, a Montgomery Ward sewing machine that I did not need, the refinanced house mortgage, a loan of $800 from his friend Elmer, and, of course, everything to do with hospital, surgery, and chemo and radiation bills as well as his funeral bill, which was now mine. I could never expect to get out of debt or imagine how much this all totaled in value. Marvin never shared about these details. I was also surprised when Stephen said, "Well, Dad wanted me to have his gun collection!" Oh, for sure, Marv never wanted me to see his guns and I had no idea where he kept the key to his huge cabinet. This presented a big problem if I gave Stephen the gun cabinet and collection PLUS one-fourth of the Erickson materials.

More blending fell apart as three of Marv's children started to contest the will. They wanted everything they thought should be theirs. In corresponding with the attorney, he said, "Yes, you can divide all of the parent and grandparent things and have Marv's sons and daughter come and get them." This process took time to arrange because I had to sort through everything in the house to make this possible.

One night when I couldn't sleep, I walked out into the living room and saw the empty chair Marv liked to sit in. I moved furniture around for a while and then decided to give the long couch and chair, which I had purchased, to Rick's family because their house had burned. The two doughboy end tables went to one of the Stene girls, who had recently married. After that I had more room to make four piles of items and try to make the piles even in value. Marvin did not want to use my china dishes, silverware, etc., when we married, so those kinds of household items that we used would be going back to his four children and I had none. Some of the items weren't worth giving or keeping.

All of this sorting helped me to decide to sell the house, because I couldn't manage the payments for the refinanced mortgage and keep up with the repairs and maintenance. One evening after getting home from work, I lifted the fiberglass, double garage door causing it to leave the track and hang halfway up and bounce a bit. The door was too high for me to kick it, so I cried a bit, which didn't hurt my foot at all!

After moving so much out of the house, it became apparent that I could never refill the empty spaces. I started to consider moving into a smaller place. I had horrible thoughts of never getting out of debt. (The debt load was staggering for several years, but by working hard, long hours, my situation did get better.)

When the sorting process was completed, I gave the four stepchildren an evening date to come and draw for their share and asked them to remove the chosen items as soon as possible. All of their family photos were laid out on the kitchen table. (Our seventeen years of pictures together I kept to put into photo albums eventually. Each stepchild received a completed album later after I got the photos copied.) Paul did not show up that evening. I had numbered the cards and the corresponding piles, so that the stepchildren could draw a number and then trade with each other if they didn't like the contents of the chosen pile, but could not trade from Paul's pile until he came for it. All of this felt like it was tearing my heart out! Marv's children were also not happy about any of this. This didn't make anyone happy!

The house had even more empty spaces after that evening. I knew for certain I had to sell the house and both Paul and Sean would have to be on their own. Some of Marvin's purchases I allowed to be repossessed and a friend wanted to take over our payments on the truck. Marvin also had five credit cards that I never knew about, which was another mess to deal with. That made me angry! Years ago when we were first married, Marv and I had agreed to use only the Wards credit card and only purchase what we needed with that. During my house search, the gun cabinet key turned up as well as some other interesting articles. Looking ahead, even though I missed Marvin greatly, I decided that when I moved into my new place I would buy a new pillow and try to leave the tears behind!

Chapter 22

NEW SONG IN MY HEART

One of my doll doctors was recuperating in Stillwater, Minnesota having had major surgery and my father had been admitted into the Baldwin Hospital (Wisconsin) with terminal heart failure, so I decided to take the afternoon off from work to bring flowers and visit with both of them. As I drove along the St. Croix River on the Minnesota side, I wept because God had given me more insight and lyrics for the song I kept hearing in my head. I never planned to "write a song," but God was very real to me! As tears streamed down my face, I was speeding in a 30 mph zone in Bayport and I wasn't aware of my car's speed.

Sound of a siren followed me until I stopped my car. "So, young lady, why were you in such a hurry?"

I answered the police officer, "I didn't even think about it, because God was revealing new words for the song that's in my head. It's about the green in your valley and the crisp snow at the bottom and how hard it is to get it just perfect without going through tough storms in life."

The officer took over while I got my papers out and wiped tears away from my eyes. I told him that my dad was dying in the Baldwin Hospital and I was taking take time off to see him. Well, this was more information than the police officer needed just to issue a speeding ticket. He read the advertisement on the trunk of my car and was writing as he asked me if I was the gal with the doll shop on the way into the city. He explained that his girlfriend collected dolls and he was interested in bringing her to my museum. Of course, I told him, "Oh, great! I'll give you a special tour."

He presented me with a warning and said, "Will you slow down when you go through my city?"

"Oh, YES, SIR! Thank you." What a nice miracle!

God gave me this song as Marv and Dad were dying:

Thank You for This Valley I Walk Through Today

Thank you for this valley I walk through today,

The darker the valley the more I learn to pray.

I found you in the flowers that were blooming by the way,

So, Lord, I thank you for this valley I walk through today.

Thank you for every hill I climb

And for every time the sun doesn't shine.

And thank you for the heartaches, hurts, and pain,

And for reminding me to bring them to Thee again and again.

Thank you for every sleepless night when I prayed

'till I knew it would be alright.
Thank you for this valley I walk through today.
Thank you for times when I'm depressed
and lonely, forgotten and alone,
And then I'm reminded that Thou art still on the throne.
Thanks for reaching down and touching my life
when it was so untouchable,
For letting me lose my life and then find it, Lord, in Thee.

Thank you for holding me when I run too fast
or cannot stand alone,
For replacing youth and beauty with peace and truth and love.
Thank you for forgiving all of yesterday's sins
and letting me start anew today.
Thank you for tapping my shoulder and saying,
"I will carry your burden, trust me, NOW!"

Life can't be all sunshine or the flowers would die,
The rivers would be barren, all desert and dry.
Life can't be all blessings or we wouldn't need to pray.
So, Lord, I thank you for this valley I walk through today.

Again I felt alone but safe in the arms of Jesus. What a mighty God I serve!

My visit with Dad was very special. He was bedridden but interested in things around him. The Baldwin, Wisconsin community was like home to him. Dad was acquainted with a lot of people coming and going in the hospital. (I think my siblings and I could be related to half of the people in that community who have Dutch ancestors.) During the visit, three of my nephews and nieces were sitting across the bed from me. Even though I know all of my relatives, to this day God has taken away the memory as to which ones were there. Once I started to witness to Dad, they were silent—but very happy for him later. I told Dad that I really needed to know where he was with Jesus because when I get to heaven I want to see him there. With the faith of a child, my father accepted Christ as his personal Savior and his name was written in the Lamb's Book of Life—forever! Great miracle!

During the last portion of my dad's life, he had to change hospitals several times so that the insurance would cover his medical expenses. Thus, he was moved back to Ramsey Hospital in St. Paul. To celebrate Dad's birthday while he stayed there, Mom wanted my huge round tray filled with chocolate "kisses"—silver-wrapped pieces around gold foil-covered pieces that had been arranged to show the number 75 in the center of the tray—his birthday number! The tray was set out at his nurse's station after we showed it to Dad. The candy was a big hit with Dad and everyone enjoyed the candy until it was all gone!

My dad was a talented man and a wonderful father. Dad didn't finish high school because as one of the oldest boys in his family, he was needed for helping with the farm work. Dad was an honest and faithful, kind and generous man. He was quick to see how things could be repaired or built to meet our family's needs. Dad conducted business with a handshake and a promise-keepers word of honor.

Mom always thought Dad was a rather "dashing" man because he usually wore his hat "cocked" to one side. He was farming when they met and later went on to become a builder and contractor.

My dad built a huge addition to our little school that included a gymnasium, lunchroom and kitchen, and classrooms for home economics and science. I actually got to use the new addition all through high school. Now there is a huge new middle school building and a large new high school north of town.

My dad also enjoyed restoring antique cars and had sixteen of them running in 1968. My folks loved to feature most of them in local parades.

When Dad died a year after Marvin died, I was committed to handling twenty-two speaking engagements. Two women on my staff agreed to fill in for me by doing one of those speeches but afterwards were quite clear about not being a featured speaker again, saying, "Absolutely no more speeches, Clare!" On the day of Dad's funeral I felt quite ill, so I stayed away from food and children and carried a plastic bag in my purse if needed. I made it through those two days and then went right back to giving speeches.

Just before my dad died in 1985, Lois—a dear friend—stopped in my shop to browse and said, "Clare, you have to tell people about Jesus and salvation because God has given you a platform for speaking. Some of those ladies won't make it to Heaven unless you tell them how to get there." I responded, "That's okay for you because you are a pastor's wife." With her finger pointed at me, she told me that she would be praying that I would speak out.

Later, while I was eating before speaking to a large group, my stomach did somersaults. I made a plea to God that I would do my best to serve Him if He would take away my nervous feelings. He heard my prayer!

For thirty-three years, I was blessed to share with audiences the history of my dolls and, best of all, my testimony of salvation, while speaking in churches and to large organizations and groups. Altogether, I have spoken to thousands of women, children, and even men. For my talks, I created a large display of a huge variety of dolls, toys, and bears on two 8 ft. long tables. As I shared my message, I wove my dolls and toys into the story. My speeches were whimsical, funny, and also serious. I have spoken at meetings in these states: Alaska, Minnesota, Wisconsin, Montana, North Dakota, South Dakota, Florida, Indiana, and Iowa.

Chapter 23

SMALL & COZY DUPLEX UP THE HILL

$\mathcal{A}$fter selling my house in Woodbury, I moved into a very comfortable, small duplex—which I rented—about five blocks from the new location of my doll hospital in Oakdale. My new home was a warm and cozy place—easy for me to entertain family and friends, and I loved decorating it.

Across the street from my home was the Tartan High School. In the early morning hours, I enjoyed hearing the band play songs and march to the beat of the drum line. I called the principal to tell him it was so great to hear and even watch the marching band practice. I think he was surprised by my phone call because he asked where I lived. Later, I learned that my landlady called frequently to tell him that the band had to practice quietly because it really bothered her.

Some wonderful friends had convinced me to relocate my doll hospital and museum into their building next to the freeway. Dave and Jerry did all of the retrofitting of the building for my shop. This new location worked well for five years. My shop was a busy place with ten to fourteen employees working most of the time. We would handle half of the passengers from a big bus in the shop and museum while the other half of the group would dine in a neighborhood restaurant before switching places.

One of my favorite dollhouse stories to share when leading visitors through the doll museum was about "Aunt Wanda" and "Uncle Walt." I based this story on my parents' dear friends who came to visit my family often when I was a young girl. I loved both of them. Uncle Walt played somewhat rough with me. Aunt Wanda often admonished him not to play so rough with my siblings and me and wear himself out! "You're not as young as you used to be you know" and on and on in a nagging, high-pitched voice she would lecture, but he would tease us anyway.

One day, Mom called from Wisconsin to say that Aunt Wanda and Uncle Walt would like to come to Oakdale that evening to see my doll museum, hospital, and shop for the first time. "Of course, they could!" I answered, while thinking that I would just skip that bedroom scene in the manor story. Mom explained that she had told them they were in a scene as two China dolls and they wanted to see it. Aunt Wanda and Uncle Walt really did love me! They felt so blessed when I started to act like them in the tour, making my voice sound like Aunt Wanda, and to show their part in the whole business of my life. Whew! Special miracle!

While I managed my shop in Oakdale, I joined the new organization Twin City Tour Managers. As a result, I spent a lot of time networking with all of the members. As the organization grew in size, my advertising expanded. Members took turns hosting the monthly meetings. Eventually, the organization became known as the Minnesota Tour Managers. My first job as a member was to serve on the Board and then to chair the first annual seminar. I met with a local graphic artist friend and asked for all his suggestions on seminars. We had heard Paul Ridgeway speak at a meeting for the local Christians in Business organization and contacted him to be the speaker for our seminar. (Years later, there wasn't anyone better for "tourism" than Paul and his Roles-Royce because of his expertise in putting together several events around the 2001 NCAA Men's Division Final Four Basketball Tournament held in Minneapolis.) The following year, I chose Paul Douglas, a talented local weather forecaster, to speak. Construction companies depended on his early morning or instant phone reports in regards to their pouring cement or other serious, huge-dollar projects. Both Paul Ridgeway and Paul Douglas were Christian men with great testimonies.

Many fine people became acquainted with my shop through doll clubs or classes. Along with running the shop, I taught classes to potential doll collectors, again held in the museum. When the class was finished, the group usually wanted to join a club. Through the years, I started twelve new clubs in the metro area and belonged to four of them at a time. The meetings were often held in my museum so the members could talk about the different dolls in my collection, which really helped the gals become grounded in making wise decisions when moving forward in building their collections. It is always delightful for me to run into one of these gals now.

The summer a doll club came to celebrate my birthday was a special time. The women were from the west side of the Minneapolis and St. Paul area. We had a delightful meal at the shop before stormy weather moved in. Then, their families called and told them to stay put because the driving conditions were pretty bad with tornado warnings and flooded roads. With that news, everyone agreed to move up to my duplex to keep the party going. We carried pillows and blankets down to my basement and began to have a great memorable evening. Some of the roads with high water were actually closed and trees were down in many places. We all ate more food and stayed up late, like when we were younger!

My days were full with working in my shop and museum, giving speeches, and starting up new doll clubs, but God opened another great door for me! Ariel called and told me she was attending the last meeting of her Missionary Alliance friends before the group would travel to the Holy Land and Switzerland. She asked me if I would ever like to go to Israel. Without hesitating, I answered, "Sure!" Ariel told me to come to the meeting to learn more about the trip and see pictures. Well, I did and had a grand time "in the Holy Land" by viewing the slides and meeting the people who would be traveling in the group. One person I met was Dorothy from North St. Paul, who made the trip sound even more appealing. For me, there was one major problem; the $200 down payment was due in a week. I told God how much I would love to go and that I knew I couldn't afford the trip. I also prayed that I would continue to serve Him and be a witness for Him. I slept well and went on working.

A local celebration in Oakdale was taking place about this time. In preparing for the annual parade, I had a huge group of children dress up as dolls or toys. In support of the community celebration, I purchased four city buttons, one for each of my judges (the doll doctors) and one for myself. What a surprise I had on the following Monday when three well-dressed business people came into my shop and presented me with a check for $200 for having THE winning button! Even though I still couldn't pay the remaining balance for the tour, I sent the down payment because this was my first sign from God.

I kept praying and trusting God for guidance regarding the trip to Israel. Just before the final payment deadline, I received a brown envelope from the government. Fully aware that I didn't owe the government any money, I let it lay unopened. When I finally opened the envelope, I found a huge check in the exact amount needed for the final down payment towards the trip. The business had been overcharged and this was a refund! Another really big miracle in my life!

Chapter 24

THE HOLY LAND TOUR—AN UNEXPECTED BLESSING!

t was 1985—a special year. Even though I greatly missed Marvin and my dad's health was failing, the Lord blessed me in several ways. One totally unexpected blessing was having the opportunity to travel with a tour group to the Holy Land.

When I arrived with the tour group in Tel Aviv that first night, "the bank" was opened as men left their small rooms and came out to exchange money.

During our stay, we had an Arab bus driver and a Jewish tour guide. Dorothy, my roommate, and I settled into a nice hotel. From there we started walking where Jesus had walked and having special devotions in many different places. Our group of about 48 people included preachers and their wives, choir directors and spouses, and some nice new friends. We sang on the bus a lot and the stories in the Bible came alive.

The second day of the tour required too much climbing for me. I had worked hard to prepare for the trip, leaving my home and my business "perfect." On the flight my ankles had become swollen, so I stayed near the bus and found the scenery around it fascinating. To be where Jesus and his followers could have walked was an overwhelming and wonderful experience, bringing tears to my eyes as I talked to God and tried to thank Him for this incredible trip.

That day, Elias, our driver, sat on a stone wall near the bus and asked me questions about the members of the tour group and where we were from. He thought it was unusual that we didn't quarrel over the seating arrangements when we got on his bus because other groups of people would do that. Elias also asked a lot questions about my family. One question in particular surprised me: "Would he look like any of my six boys and fit into my family?" I replied, "Yes, you could fit in because three of them have very dark brown eyes." Elias had been observing all of us in his upper mirror and was obviously formulating opinions that came out again later.

The tour was packed with stops that related to the history of the Bible and entertainment events that kept us going long hours each day. On the seventh day, Elias invited my friends Amy and Karen to have coffee with him in his room after we unloaded the bus. Men are men! I suggested that Amy and Karen have coffee with Elias in the hotel bar/drink area instead of his room. The coffee was next to "medical mud" and so strong we needed a lot of cream, which wasn't available. We had a few minutes to pray together and I encouraged Amy and Karen to witness to Elias.

(Before the tour, everyone was told to use the word "believers" instead of born again.) It was decided that I would be a prayer partner to Amy and Karen and we would meet after their time with Elias.

As I walked through the lobby to return to my room, Elias was waiting to invite me also. (My nose came back into joint.) I accepted the invitation, saying that I would be pleased to join him. Within that short time, God opened a door to lead Elias to the saving knowledge of Christ. Great Holy Land miracle!

We asked the local missionary's wife if we could buy a Bible for Elias and have her mark the verses we had used. She and her husband actually donated a nice large Bible, which read from the back to the front, of course.

The next evening after a busy day we quietly presented him with his own Bible out in front of his bus and he beamed with pride and joy while holding it for a photo. The following day as we toured through Cana in Galilee he told us his wife and three children would board the bus and walk through it to meet us. What a pleasure that was for us!

Some members of our tour group planned some special things for the "banquet" night during the tour. Winnie had suggested I bring balloons and narrow rings of rolled up party paper to add to the gaiety. I started to collect the ends of toilet tissue to make large bows. This paper was similar to our crepe paper but in subdued colors. After the banquet, the waiters asked if they could have the balloons and laughed and pointed to the big paper bows I made with the toilet tissue.

During the banquet while sitting at a table with a wonderful couple from South Dakota, I visited with the man next to me, talking about the tour and learning about his family and his faith. I inquired about when he had accepted Christ as his Savior and found out that he had not done that! His answer left me with a big, overwhelming "daaah" feeling. I talked about the importance of that decision and how he had to make that decision for himself, even though he had two choices for where to spend eternity— heaven or hell. I told him, "Don't put it off." I thought everybody on that trip was born again and so was surprised by his answer. As soon as I could, our visiting went back to discussing his huge farming operation and equipment. That evening, his wife became a dear friend and told me how blessed she felt to have someone else care enough to witness to her husband. That's my job! After I accepted Christ as my Savior, I wanted to do my part for that wonderful, forever partnership. Within a few months after the Holy Land tour, she wrote to me to say that her husband had accepted Christ as his Savior. A South Dakota miracle!

Later that summer, I invited the whole tour group to meet at a nearby restaurant for lunch and then gave them a tour of my doll hospital, shop, and museum. We spent a lot of time sharing photos and reminiscing while eating. Making and sharing memories with friends is quite special!

Elias, the Arab bus driver, became a believer!
Wonderful miracle!

On the 1985 trip to Israel, Clare rode a camel twice—
neither time was graceful!

Chapter 25

MINNESOTA ARTIST AT THE
MINNEAPOLIS INSTITUTE OF ART

 s the number of visitors—young girls and older adults—
to my museum grew, I continued to keep busy creating
doll scenes and conducting tours. One spring day in 1988, three
well-dressed gentlemen from the Minneapolis Institute of Art (MIA)
stopped in, so I gave them a tour of the museum. We were about half
way talking about the displays when they asked if I would be one
of the Minnesota artists highlighted in a special exhibit, displaying
my dolls in a large "round" dollhouse. I tried to explain that I wasn't
an artist; however, when they pointed out the little plate with very
small cookies on it and said that's what they wanted, I was persuaded.
"OH, OKAY!" I agreed. As the conversation continued, I suggested a
rectangular dollhouse 16 ft. long by 10 ft. high, making it the largest
in the world. I thought that shape would be easier for visitors to relate
to than a round one. I was extremely excited to have the honor of
furnishing that dollhouse. At that time, the largest dollhouse (and
also the most valuable) was Colleen Moore's dollhouse in Chicago.

The largest dollhouse in the world at the Art Institute came to be called the Erickson manor. The structure was built in a huge showroom that was entirely black. Huge spotlights illuminated the dollhouse in that dark room. To enter the room, visitors had to open a screen door, hearing that familiar sound from days gone by.

While I was decorating each room in the dollhouse with "Victorian" wallpaper, Stewart asked me if I would like to keep the house when the show was over. I remarked, "Not really! I couldn't put it back together after it all came apart." He quickly thought of a solution and said, "Oh, we can take the attic off and cut the house down the middle. You would have to move the sections on two big trucks." I gave that suggestion some thought and devised a plan. (YES! THANKS!)

The Minnesota Artists Exhibition Program gave me the privilege to share a giant dollhouse filled with scenes of early 20th century life in miniature. The MIA staff sought to expand the traditional definitions of artist and artwork in a new direction by featuring creative work by people who see special value in objects and feel a personal connection with them. This went beyond collecting for the artists showing skills to restore and preserve, write articles, organize clubs and teach classes, offer performances and fashion their lives around the objects of their passion. The work of six Minnesotan artists was featured.

While my dolls were on display for eight weeks, I spent three days a week at the Art Institute, wearing my Victorian costume and talking to people about the family who "lived" in the Erickson

Manor. (Marvin, having died, wasn't included in my dollhouse stories.) What an honor it was to be the storyteller who kept visitors engaged in what they saw and heard!

During the time leading up to that exhibit, my stories blossomed as my business "Antie Clare's" Doll Hospital, Shop & Museum became better known. Initially, Marvin had helped me start the business and even collected articles for my doll museum. I wish that he could have enjoyed the excitement of having "Antie Clare" and her dolls featured in the Art Institute.

When the show closed, the empty Erickson manor was moved out and stored in a pole barn on a farm in Afton, Minnesota because it wouldn't fit in my shop. Later in 1988, my business was moved to a large new space; then the Erickson manor had a new home. A fun miracle!

Clare in costume, standing with four of the five other Minnesota artists

The "largest dollhouse in the world" built at the Minneapolis Institute of Art. Clare decorated and filled its seven rooms and attic space with her antique dolls and named it the Erickson Manor. On weekends for two months, Clare shared her dollhouse stories about life in the olden days.

Chapter 26

THE BIGGEST & THE BEST

$\mathcal{T}$oward the end of the five-year lease for my shop in Oakdale, the owners asked me to move out. They planned to use the acre of land for a more lucrative business concern. So, I started the search for a new location. It seemed best to hire my staff to pack, label, and move boxes, and set up everything again at the new site. For the move, I would have to plan carefully and have supplies and food for those helping.

One day, Patti—one of my seamstresses—told me about a big, former bank building in North St. Paul, which had been vacant for two years. It was over 3,000 square feet and I also learned that I could live in part of the building. I was thrilled to have enough space to set up the dollhouse, which had been displayed at the Minneapolis Institute of Art. I also envisioned the display that Johnny Fesendine would set up—his huge Steiff German Village. A lot of space would be needed to show everything in Johnny's village. There were seventeen automated figures, such as a man fishing and another one loading grain, as well as three miniature buildings, and a village pump that had running water. I remember thinking that my stories should be built around Bill Sandberg, the Burgermeister, Doctor Broman and his wife and their sons, and business people in my new city, North St. Paul.

The details were all worked out. "Antie Clare's" Doll Hospital, Shop & Museum was moved to Seppala Boulevard in North St. Paul. In the new location, there was enough room for my apartment, the museum, salesroom, doll hospital, large business office, and even storage in the basement! Gary, the owner, and his son, Tom, cleared and remodeled the former bank building for the shop and built a small apartment, which I decorated in a charming Victorian style. I was excited to be able to showcase the largest dollhouse in the world and my new job was to insure John's village and enjoy the displays with hundreds of tourists.

A lot of work had to be done before the dollhouse could be seen by the public. As the house parts arrived in my shop, were reconnected, and prepared for the new location, Sue, my dear friend, wallpapered most of the Erickson manor rooms. Her mom happened to call while Sue was sitting in an upstairs bedroom, so Sue told her that she had wallpapered five rooms in Antie Clare's house that night!

In 1981, my folks had given me about 700 dolls and accessories when I first started my business. Still, I was even more deeply touched by their generosity and continued support for my business when they donated their "Victorian collectibles," like a huge baby buggy, several mannequins, and other items, to my museum at its biggest and best location in North St. Paul.

For the grand opening of my shop, I was given big bolts of red nylon, rain-proofed material that must have been 250 feet long because the wide red "ribbon" reached around the entire building. I had a huge red bow displayed on each of the four entrance doors. Someone else gave me rolls of patriotic bunting that we used to decorate the tables set outside to draw attention to our sales for Crazy Days and Fall Roundup.

Mom was able to be with me for the grand opening of my shop and other events in North St. Paul. When the next Mayor's Prayer Breakfast came up, the planning committee asked me to speak at their event, so the business community got to know I was a Christian woman, in business, in their town! What a marvelous beginning!

The new location for my shop was great! I lived in my precious apartment in the same building as the business, right on the main street and at the corner with the semaphore light. Many business people would drop in to ask questions, but the three bar owners located around my business preferred to have live dolls!

My grandchildren, Ryan and Hillary, spent a lot of time with me in the shop on Seppala Boulevard when they were young. They learned to use my doll hospital equipment, especially the airbrush to paint anything and the sewing machine to create outfits. Their uncle Sean had already worked for me. Sean also loved to create with the airbrush and was a winner of trips and money for his garish costumes.

As an adult, Ryan became friends with members of a "tall" bike club. He kept putting bicycle parts together to make tall bikes and rode with the club all over Minneapolis and out to St. Croix River, which flowed between the borders of Wisconsin and Minnesota. For one trip, I suggested the bike-club members stop at my shop to rest. I talked to Sean about providing cookies and lemonade for the riders. He advised against having lemonade but instead providing tap water without ice cubes. The day came and I picked up several boxes of large cookies. (I spent about $150.) I had notified the police about who, what, and how long the bikers would be there.

When the tall bike club arrived, the bikers were hot, sweaty, and exhausted. There were about ninety young adults with all kinds of bicycles. Their tall bikes filled our parking lot and the park across the street. The cookies disappeared fast and each biker had a large plastic cup for water for refilling. Occasionally, someone would dump a cup of water over his head with a huge sigh of relief. Some of the bikers actually just used my hose and stood under the running water to cool down. My staff kept filling the large container with water until everyone was cared for. Many of the bikers walked into my air-conditioned shop to cool off and look around. A cool miracle! My staff interacted with the bikers and we answered a lot of questions. This commotion of bikers shook up the town and neighbors. Before long, there was a parade of curious people gathered around us to check out the bikers. My favorite photographer Linda Baumister arrived to take photos for our local paper. I hosted this refreshment stop for five years—more bikers and more cookies each year!

My staff reached twenty-two in number at this location. With more doll doctors on staff, we accepted more extensive and complicated restoration projects of dolls, bears, figurines, statues, and lamps. The photography projects increased and improved, especially later with having a great Web site presence. The Internet was a great outreach as my business became international as merchandise was sold on E-bay. Thanks to the help of those who did a marvelous job with improving and updating my Web site.

The record keeping and office work for the business grew as did my involvement in the association, Christians in Business; North St. Paul businesses; the historic society; Crazy Days and Fall Roundup events; and the Minnesota Tour Managers.

I had collected costumes since being involved in Cub Scouts with my sons and was active in the business sector of North Saint Paul for twenty-one years. Some friends and I would dress up in Western style or as Victorian families and ride in a stagecoach (belonged to a friend of my folks) from Roberts, Wisconsin. I counted on the children in my life to ride with us in the local parades. We were filmed and featured on local TV news programs when reporters told about the parade.

When I was president of the North St. Paul Business Association, I tried to make the "largest snowman in the world" a familiar landmark. The concrete snowman was only about a block away from my shop. I owned a chubby snowman suit and decided to have family and friends wear it during community events. With some trial and error, my son Sean and grandson Ryan were the first snowmen.

Keith, a friend, became the best snowman ever for about sixteen years and represented North Saint Paul faithfully at all events—meetings, special occasions, royal events, and parades. During one local parade, young Michael (a friend's son) was standing on top of the stagecoach and Keith, as the snowman, was walking alongside it in the White Bear Avenue parade. When the driver stopped the stagecoach abruptly, the boy fell off onto the blacktop street. Keith (a former paramedic) ripped off his round "snow" head. The crowd gasped, being surprised by seeing who was wearing the suit. Keith assisted Michael, who stood up and was okay but had the yellow street line on his white shirt. A Michael miracle! For the first Gold Plate Dinner, Keith, the snowman, sat on a gal's lap. She felt his chest to see if the person in costume was a girl or guy. It took quite awhile for the town folk to eliminate those they thought were wearing the suit!

I remember the day when Monica (now Greg's wife) came into my doll shop and said she would like to be my princess for the Miss North St. Paul contest. I had met her once before and couldn't think of her name at the time, so I said, "Please sit down and tell me about yourself." Of course, I accepted her request! Monica was a beautiful young lady and I was blessed to have her also help me with the Historical Luncheon and Style Show during Heritage Days. For the style show, she gave the planning committee ten decades of music on ten cassettes for short introductions. As emcee, I shared historical facts about our city while twenty-five women and children wore the appropriate outfits for the decades. I had bribed Greg into helping each model step on and off the elevated ramp by saying, "OK, I'll get a tux for you." When Monica came out, he followed her and then walked over to me wanting to know who she was. The next time she came out, Greg asked me to give him her phone number. I told him to get it himself and that was the beginning of their romance and, later, marriage.

The morning after Monica and Greg's first date, he called me to ask for a favor. He wanted me to order long stemmed red roses and have them sent with a card to Monica at work. So, that's what I did, even though I was just as busy at work as Greg was!

Through the years, I collected and filled a huge drawer of memorabilia from the Minneapolis Institute of Art exhibit; the operation of the doll hospital, shop, and museum; involvement in business organizations, and items related to my public speaking engagements: magazine articles, local newspaper articles, and photos; plus many television and radio interviews and speeches on video. The Lord blessed me in many different ways that filled my life with rich memories as I met so many wonderful people.

Clare standing in her shop at the Oakdale location

The talented doll doctors at work in "Antie Clare's" Doll Hospital

The Steiff German village featured seventeen automated figures, three large buildings, and running water.

Clare being interviewed on KTIS radio by Joyce Harley and Wayne Peterson in Crossroads Chapel at the Minnesota State Fair

"Antie Clare" partying with precious Henslins and cousins

Christina (on the right) stands with three large hard-
plastic dolls dressed for winter, looking at a toy-store
window display in the museum. She never talked to the
dolls, just enjoyed the scene.

Chapter 27

A BRIEF HISTORY OF NORTH ST. PAUL

s a businesswoman and resident of North St. Paul for many years, I always enjoyed sharing facts about this wonderful, amazing city. I led trolley tours on two special occasions through the neighborhoods and told the groups the following information:

North St. Paul became a city in 1887 and is young compared to London, which was founded 400 years before Christ. North St. Paul was about Henry Castle and his wife, Margaret. Their children were James, (who died first) Harry, Charles, Margaret, Anne, Mary, and Helen. This gentleman was rather unique! After retiring as a Civil War captain, Henry moved from the East Coast to Illinois and then later to St. Paul. In 1873 he was a member of the Minnesota State Legislature. Three years later, he combined politics with journalistic talents. Henry and some friends purchased the *St. Paul Dispatch*. He was the editor, publisher, and president of the company for ten years. He resigned to become a land developer. His first town site was south and east of Silver Lake called Castle. It was incorporated seven years later and renamed North Saint Paul.

Capt. Henry Castle planned North St. Paul to be progressive and today we plan to keep it progressive. Henry Ansom Castle was a very ambitious gentleman with a great vision. He started industries and built 100 cottages that first year to make North St. Paul a working man's city comparable to Chicago. In the early 1880s the recovering national financial depression attracted waves of immigrants to this community and supplied the labor market for Capt. Castle's plans.

As a prolific author, Henry A. Castle wrote many books, including *The History of St. Paul & Vicinity* and *Minnesota, It's Story and Biography*. He also produced weekly articles for the *Saturday Evening Post* and *Collier's Weekly* and monthly articles for *Harper's Magazine* and *McClure's Magazine*. Capt. Castle was also an ardent speaker. A member of the Republican Party, he spoke for party candidates and at community celebrations and civic events. He was wounded during the war and later injured by a car while crossing the street in St. Paul. Henry was almost 75 years old when he died. Margaret died shortly thereafter.

Main Street has seen many changes from wooden sidewalks and center islands to landscaping and handicap accessible sidewalks. The corner of 7th & Seppala Boulevard was also the area where a water trough had been located to accommodate the horses coming into town many, many years ago. Seppala appeared to be an alley;

however, it was named after a barber and is a boulevard. The St. Paul streetcars would travel on the tracks through North St. Paul on the way to Wildwood Amusement Park at the south end of White Bear Lake.

Until a few years ago, many yellow brick buildings on the five-acre site just east of Helen Street made up the Luger Furniture Company. The Luger family had moved the manufacturing of furniture from Wabasha, Minnesota to North St. Paul by building a new factory there in 1887. The smokestack for the factory reached 86 feet and the company employed thirty to forty Luger family members, sixty factory workers, and six traveling agents. The business survived the 1880s depression. At the company's peak, workers filled one carload of furniture a day.

For many years, the railroad was the lifeline of this city, enabling manufacturers to sell products all over the central and western states. Four to five trains stopped each day at our freight house and depot.

Today, the beautiful Gateway State Trail (a converted 18-mile rail trail) runs from the Lake Phalen area through North St. Paul to Stillwater. This trail may someday be connected with other trails to allow cyclists and hikers to continue on to the Willard Munger State Trail that runs from Hinckley to Duluth and then travel on the North Shore State Trail. North St. Paul's goal was to sow wild flower seed along its area of the Gateway Trail.

North High School is one of six schools in our community. In 1916, Henry Castle laid that building's cornerstone and died later that year.

Also on the "Tour of North Saint Paul" would be the landmark St. Mark's Lutheran Church. This church was built on the site of the all grades, three-story school building, which had a circular slide escape from the upper story. Years ago on a clear day all over the city, you could hear the bells playing hymns from the church steeple.

It is important to keep in mind that in the 19th century this area was a wooded land with rolling meadows. The Dakota Indian Reservation was located west of this area. Today many streets are named Shawnee, Chippewa, Mohawk, Indian Way, and Apache. The Native Americans needed Silver Lake and the St. Croix River for a source of food, an abundance of fish and cranberry bogs.

Silver Lake (18 feet deep) was and is a very busy lake for residents to walk, play, swim, fish, boat, water ski, picnic, and ice skate. In 1934 the drought was so severe that the lake was nearly dried up. City records also indicate that it was 110 degrees on June 1, and then in 1942 with the abundance of rain, the lake flooded.

There are also some special historical houses in North St. Paul. The residence on 2609 E. 18th Avenue is the only octagon house in Ramsey County. The house was built in 1887. It had four porches, several marble fireplaces, and much hand-painted woodwork. The house was built for the Joseph E. Osborn family. In the early 1890s the country entered a recession and the house went back to the builder. The next owner of the house was Ernest Reiff, who also bought the Casket Company and became president of that business. The house has been known as the Reiff House or called Woodbine.

The trees along 7th Avenue are some of the 10,000 planted in 1887. Examples of the North St. Paul Cottage Company homes can still be seen today. When first built, they were each sold for a $50 down payment. House numbers 2638, 2640, 2644, 2662 and 2666 are original cottages. The houses on 8th Avenue with numbers 2689, 2697, and 2701 were built by Luger family members for their homes.

In the early years of the 1900's, industry was bustling. Besides Luger Furniture, other factories made bobsleds, skis, wagons, fishing tackle, organs, pianos, sleighs, furniture and caskets. With incandescent lamps, factories could remain open longer than daylight hours. They also had carpenters hired to complete one cottage a day before winter set in. Other businesses and interests included the iron works, saddles, harnesses and collars, agriculture, White Pine lumber mills, grain merchandising, and flour milling.

Once the grandest of residential hotels, the Morton House was the finest of buildings with owners who held superb dinners and gala balls. A streetlight was on this corner with a red light to be turned on for the fire wagon, pulled by horses. The telephone operator flashed it for the police and fire department to see and call in. In the winter, a skating rink was flooded in front of the hotel for the community to use.

Places of business have changed over the years. As the city grew, we had Keindel's meat, groceries, and produce, which later closed as the Jubilee Store. Miller Shoe Store was known for very good quality shoes in many sizes. A devastating fire caused many shoes to be thrown out onto the main street years ago. The former brick bank building became an antique shop and then adjacent buildings were elegantly refurbished for the K & J Catering Co. Mac's Dinette was always fun to eat in or take friends there for a meal. Since 1937 it has been known for great breakfasts, lunches, and historical photographs.

In 1911, 1933, and 1936 there were great fires in the city and limited equipment. In 1997, the city was able to boast about magnificent up-to-date emergency equipment and a partial volunteer fire department. Auto repair shops and even a dealer, lawyers, fun shops and antique shops and a mall, an auctioneer, printer, barbers, beauty salons, Anderson Cabinets, many churches, dry cleaners, and computer sales—all can be found in North St. Paul.

Neumann's Bar is said to be the oldest continuous bar in Minnesota (been serving customers since 1887) and still has giant live frogs in the window. Hamm's Brewery installed a magnificent mahogany bar when the business opened, the ancient cash register, and old furniture, like a museum.

The Post Office building has three panel murals painted by Donald Humphrey called "Production." This mural depicts sturdy, rural figures during the depression. As part of the New Deal WPA program, our Post Office was chosen to be the location for this commission. Mr. Humphrey has permanent works at the New York Metropolitan Museum. The North St. Paul Post Office was the first to incorporate C.O.D. and Rural Delivery while Henry Castle was in the Postal Service.

Some famous people of North St. Paul include Jerry Bell, the Minnesota Twins president; Frank Sanders, ski jumper; and Doctor Cowren, who had much to do with the discovery and cure for chicken pox and shingles. The births of over 1,200 babies were recorded in Dr. Cowren's journals—the amount charged, received or paid in produce, or not paid for. Henry Castle's daughter painted the lady slipper, which became the Minnesota state flower. Members of the Luger family were the builders and members of the Berwall family were roofers. As mayor, Bill Sandberg, was a great leader for our city and had more photos in the Review and Historical Museum than anyone else.

The Sandberg Mortuary has been a family business for many years. When Bill Sandberg was the mayor, he had salvation scripture on his car license plate, which surprised and blessed me. Mayor Sandberg is our most photographed and recorded person in today's history at the museum.

Whenever I led a tour group, I always liked to take visitors to see the city's snowman—the tallest one in the world—which was built in 1972–74 by Gary Mulcahy, Lloyd Kusling, and other men. The concrete stucco snowman weighs 20 tons and is 18 to 21 feet wide and about 44 feet tall. His smile is 6 feet wide.

The snowman was created for the annual community celebration, Sno-Daze, and can be viewed from Highway 36.

The North St. Paul Historical Society was founded as an association in 1979. For over 21 years the Society sponsored the Annual Ice Cream Social held on the south and east shores of Silver Lake. The Bald Eagle Water Ski Club performed during the event. Ice cream cones were sold and the antique car show was enjoyed as well as the band performance, prizes, games, and plenty of food, and good weather!

Capt. Castle's dream of a workingman's community has grown and seen many changes for over 100 years. Industrial buildings and railroads have been replaced by streamlined highways, a bicycle trail, rolling hills, a dozen or more parks, and fountains.

Wouldn't the early settlers of this community laugh and smile to see that we have a historical museum that holds a collection of papers, photographs, and objects that tell about them and the changes in our community.

I praise God for the people with a vision, positive personalities, leaders, and givers, who built their dreams and provided service to others for better living. You may have ancestors recorded in the cemeteries located in North St. Paul. If so, your roots are long and deeply embedded in this community.

St. Paul Winter Carnival at the "Largest Snowman" in the world
(North St. Paul)

Miss North St. Paul and her court (1994–95) with Mr.
Snowman (Keith) and Clare

Chapter 28

I MISS MOM FOR THE MILLION THINGS SHE IS TO ME

While traveling back to New Richmond, Wisconsin, one day, I felt like my world was coming down on me again. A major worry, my health issues were slowing me down at work. I remember thinking that I need to accept the fact that the world is not falling apart at the feet of Jesus. He has plans all laid out for it, for me, for us! Where does one get on or leave off? Do we lose faith going through hardships? Maybe we don't have faith before the hard times? Jesus didn't leave us with fear, loneliness, guilt, and failure. I don't have to win here; God does. So I must keep serving and living for Jesus.

After having major abdominal surgery, I spent time with Mom in New Richmond so that I wouldn't be in the shop doing work too soon. Mom and I watched all four films in her favorite Little Women series and really enjoyed them. When she got the flu, I offered to speak to her nursing home people one afternoon. Sitting down and doing my own "show and tell" with a small doll and my folks' wedding picture, I made up a speech that involved all of them. Everyone seemed to enjoy my presentation.

Later, when my Mom was dying, I needed to spend the night back at the apartment. About 6 a.m. in the morning I rolled over in bed and sniffed smoke. I jumped up and started to check appliances, finding out that everything I turned on spit and blew a fuse or spit and spit and killed the radio, television, and computer. Calling the city to see if some guys were working on the building, I was told "No" but someone would come to check it. (I made a dash for my bathrobe!) Six city workers arrived and directed me to turn everything off so that they could examine every electrical thing in the place.

It was discovered that the fluorescent lights in my little kitchen had a short out in the ballast, which was slow burning. Smoke rolled out when the workers got into the ceiling. Well, the owner blamed it on me and said he wouldn't pay for any of the appliances or problems. The brave city worker said the owner should pay for all building problems because that was not my instigation. By 8:30 in the morning, I had articulated THE problems and what I could do next to get back to Mom and the relatives.

Mom clung to her life until my sister Winnie and her husband came from North Dakota and my son Douglas arrived from Alaska. It was her 88th birthday and her favorite choir of gals came to sing in the hallway outside of her room. Of course, other residents complained about the noise, so everyone squeezed into her room. Her pastor arrived and we all shifted once again so that about thirty-eight of us stood in there. Having come out of her coma earlier that day, Mom had a great message for us. She talked about the importance in accepting Jesus and to love Him and serve Him. She asked her pastor to pray and wanted all of us to hold hands. "Squeezed" together, knowing how hard it was for us to hold hands, you would have raised your eyebrows and smiled. Later in the day, Mom slipped into another coma and died on her 88th birthday in October 1998.

My wonderful parents lived all of their lives within a 20-mile radius of where they were born. It was no surprise that they had many friends; so many people knew them all of their lives. My folks were great role models and had compassionate hearts.

My siblings and I know Mom was born again at age nineteen when playing the piano in her church in Hammond, Wisconsin and is now with her Savior. What we do find hard is when both parents have died, the family celebrations and holidays change. Family gatherings are downsized. Some family members have moved out of the area and our children are going through what we did and have to make choices of where they go to celebrate during the year. Precious memories of my parents!

Chapter 29

MOVING WEST TO ROSEVILLE

"*A*ntie Clare's" Doll Hospital, Shop & Museum on Seppala Boulevard had been a bustling business for almost 18 years when the building owner broke my lease in 2004. He kept telling me I could move to his smaller location one block behind the main street, which was his option. The owner had made plans to have my former large space be used for a more lucrative business.

My business was for sale for three years and it was interesting that because it looked like so much fun one should be rich quickly! Thirteen possibilities responded and some were really unusual—almost wacky. Two individuals came together and I showed them around and gave them information papers as they left. The next day I received a call from them. They wanted to know if they could buy a new car and house in a year if they purchased my business. I smirked a muffled chuckle and answered that they may purchase anything they can afford because I do not know about their financial status.

The Steiff German Village had to go home with Johnny Fesendine and I also returned other visiting exhibits in the museum. All of the Plexiglass fronts had to come off the displays and I began to price all of the dolls and articles in my collection exhibited in the doll museum.

I had been able to pay my rent but was behind on some bills. On the day of the sale my banker and his wife wanted to help so they volunteered to handle the transactions. I also had an auction. By that time the doll hospital and supplies had been moved to the building owner's new location behind the main street after retrofitting it. Great staff! We settled as quickly as possible. With this mess going on, "Antie Clare's" Doll Hospital still received and sent home restoration projects to please our customers.

It was my job to pack up the contents of my apartment and prepare to move my personal stuff as soon as possible. I began the search for a new apartment and the first people I called were located in Roseville. They were surprised because I was the first to respond. They showed me the duplex rental property within a couple of hours. I loved it as an affordable two-bedroom unit with a fireplace, storage area, laundry in the basement, and a small garage for my car!

My son Greg and my church guys helped me move my "apartment" to this nice duplex. It seemed like I was up all hours settling in both places. I didn't have time to be exhausted, but I was hurting because my life was extremely challenging. It broke my heart to think that my plans were so great but not working out the way I had hoped. It was the third time I was evicted! It seemed like I was being treated unfairly! The Beanie Baby Co. had strapped me into huge quantities not ordered and a special VISA they took advantage of. Our order was only what my customers wanted so I wouldn't crowd my small place with them. We had about 300 customers. My great staff sorted the orders and I called for pick-ups with no one standing in line to push and shove.

My world was falling down at my feet! In desperation, I realized I was busy, healthy, and alone; my sons were busy working and traveling; and I just kept trying to organize all the necessary plans. I always thought my plans would work because they were my desires for the business and myself. But God had His plans for me and He could change my direction to stop this havoc.

Yes, the Holy Spirit was there, but I wasn't using Him as my anchor! Thus, I started to depend on God more and go back to His Word to clear my direction. I needed courage to obey God, slowing down and listening to Him. I came to the realization that God was asking me if I really liked this messy pace OR did I want His best for me. It was a special blessing to have several born again ladies on my staff. As I slowed down and went back to staying close to my Savior, they were a great help. I even started to plan for retirement when I learned Highway 36 would be closed for road improvements.

I personally like to be neat and coordinated and look my best even for moving and when shopping for supplies to represent my business and myself as a Christian. With more prays, going to

Scripture, and claiming the promises I already knew, a new zeal and purpose in my heart resulted. There still were special speaking engagements for me to handle and this too came alive.

In October of 2007, the staff finished and returned "patients" (restoration projects) and worked to help me close the business. The evening before my final business day, I drove all around North St. Paul and counted seventeen vacant business buildings—some were much larger than the space I had for my doll hospital.

The end of my business came. My car was crammed full and I was almost ready to leave and run errands. With my last load in my arms, I tripped on the concrete, dropping everything, hitting my head, breaking my glasses, scraping my face, hurting my right arm, and bruising my right knee, which began to swell up. After turning in the key for the building, I headed home and spent the following week icing those sore spots and relaxing.

When I arrived at home the landlord was in my kitchen, having moved my hutch and table out of his way, and was cutting a big oval hole in the floor to construct a spiral stairway to the basement. This was the last thing I needed because the other stairs were so much easier for me to use. He said my rent would be increasing $400 more a month and in my stupor I tried to look desperate and huffed a bit and said I would have to move after I regrouped!

Also on that day, Highway 36 closed for six months, which actually turned into a year. My business couldn't have survived that closure!

Chapter 30

FURTHER WEST IN ROSEVILLE

his was what God had for my next blessing! After having made the decision to retire, I started the search for a one-bedroom apartment. Almost immediately I signed a lease for an apartment unit in Roseville that had a small bedroom and balcony facing east. Greg helped me move in as soon as it was ready. How grateful I am for the help of friends, co-workers, and my sons!

Soon after, a feeling of guilt over retiring started to weigh heavily on me. One day, Winnie admonished me to get over it. She asked, "You have worked how many years? (About 60) Well, you deserve to enjoy life now."

My current residence is in a large brick building that has three wings of four floors each. There would be about 140 residents in the complex when the apartments are full. Rules and regulations came with the key to my apartment and so did the smell of cooking as you walk through the hallways.

While living here, I have enjoyed many new experiences and have met many fine people. After I got settled in my new apartment, I worked on puzzles in the community room, exercised, and did crafts along with other special events.

The Red Cross Blood Center was closer to where I lived, so I signed up to be a regular giver. After about a year of being a donor, I was asked if I would give platelets. They told me it would take about two hours and I could watch a film while I was donating. So, I became an "apheresis angel" for two more years.

During late June and early July of 2010, Greg's family and Doug's family provided me with a two-week tourist vacation in the Anchorage, Alaska area. What a trip that was! The visit with Douglas and his wife, Tessie, and my dear friends was filled with many wonderful memories and better than I could have imagined.

Doug and Tessie usually spend two weeks hunting caribou north of Kotzebue and will fill three freezers if it is a good hunt. Tessie is a talented cook so during my visit we enjoyed eating her many ways of cooking caribou. Also on that trip I went for a "dogsled" ride, which was actually on wheels. (Twice before on previous trips it wasn't possible.) What a delightful time that was! The people who owned the "dogsleds" also owned ninety sled dogs. When the first dog was attached to the trailer for hookup, the rest of the pack went crazy, like they were saying, "I want to go, too!" With so much barking, it was really noisy, but when the sled dogs were running, they were almost quiet. One female dog had given birth to seven puppies the day before we arrived, so we got to hold them. The puppies have a little "thumb" type knob on the inside of their front paws. After we left, the owners removed these knobs to prevent injuries so they would never get caught on a limb or be torn off later.

My second earthquake experience happened on that trip while staying with Doug and Tessie in Anchorage. One evening while we sat watching the news in their living room, I saw their neighbor's house move quite a bit, followed next by the trees, and then I was moving. Feeling quite surprised and puzzled, I asked, "What is going on now?" They calmly watched me to see if I would panic and said, "It's an earthquake, Mom." According to the news report, the epic center was ninety miles east of where I was staying and closer to Whittier in Prince William Sound.

In Anchorage, we visited museums, shops, tourist places and even garage sales. Our friends, Jim and Katie LaBau picked me up and we spent a day eating as well as dragging out scads of memories. Jim had written many professional papers and traveled to speak for the Forest Service at conference meetings. He received high national awards before retiring from the Forest Service.

Doug and Tessie collect Alaskan artifacts; their home is almost a museum. While visiting them, I have sewn drapes and curtains for their home and added black material to the back of their bedroom curtains to help Doug, Tessie, and their family sleep better during the long summer days. I could read a book without lights until 11:30 p.m.! It was quite fascinating to see their vegetable garden because their produce is always much larger in size than what is grown here in Minnesota due to the longer daylight hours. I saw huge cabbages and large carrots and heads of lettuce, too.

Even today, Doug and Tessie let me know (with snickers) when their weather is warmer than mine in Minnesota. The "Japan Current," also called Kuroshio Current, does bring some warmth with it for them. I am blessed to hear from them often by telephone.

Sean, my youngest son, and I also have a close bond today, which was in place through many parts of my life. Sean was four years old when the boys and I left Alaska to live in Wisconsin. Throughout his life, Sean has had a pleasing, winsome personality. Always a happy, helpful, and kind person, Sean has had many friends. In fact, today his friends would say if Sean calls for a get-together, bonfire, or "bash" about sunset, there could be 50–100 friends and friends of friends gathering at his place.

Sean's interest in "arts and crafts" exploded as he experimented with a vast variety of "what can I do with this?" projects. While living at home and working in my doll hospital, Sean became very familiar with the equipment and supplies I used. Yet his skills blossomed beyond the kind of projects handled in the doll hospital. His quest for more artistic experiences was strong as he encouraged and persuaded me to learn to do this and that—which he had mastered—while I managed my business and even today. Sean's skills have surpassed mine, so I am his "VIP Mom" and cheerleader and am not surprised by the latest grandiose idea he has to share. His abilities and talented craftsmanship have opened a door to the world for him with Japan being a favorite destination as well as Alaska.

I have thought about the time when Sean, as a six year old, attended Vacation Bible School. This opened the door to his salvation as well as mine and to many more in my family.

I have lived in my current home for a while now and am always excited to talk to acquaintances about my relationship with my Savior. I remember one day in particular: a sweet little lady named Henrietta came and stood by me while I was spending time in the community room. I asked if she wanted to talk to me and found out that she did. So, we moved to a quiet corner in the room to visit. Within a few minutes, she accepted Christ. (I was thrilled!) Henrietta told me how happy she was and walked out of the room with a big smile on her face. Two weeks later, Henrietta had to be hospitalized and she died. What a miracle of eternal joy! (Five other women who live here also have accepted Christ, for which I praise the Lord!) Forgiven people are going to Heaven. Everyone has a choice to make: HEAVEN or HELL —both are eternal!

Chapter 31

MEMORIES OF EXCITING ADVENTURES

Through the years, many other interesting things have happened to me. This includes the time when I was asked to be the International Doll Doctor at the Festival of Nations in 2002 at the Excel Center in St. Paul. I had to set up a booth for sales, wear a costume, and take a few dolls in for restoration.

For many years I had the privilege and joy of arranging flowers for our church auditorium. One day Pastor Bruce walked through the auditorium when I was arranging the flowers up front and said, "Hey! I just heard you for the third time today giving your "Christian in Business" testimony about serving God in the marketplace on KTIS radio." As he left he said, "Hmm, Christians ought to serve God even as a customer in the marketplace."

The members of Metro Woman's Center Board asked if I would join their organization. One of the pregnant moms needed a home to go to after she released her baby for adoption, so I answered, "YES!" to both requests. We do lots of praying for the many needs this presents. It has been my pleasure to serve on that Board in the

Twin Cities for more than thirteen years. The donations received by the organization have been used to purchase the house, known as Amazing Grace Home, for unwed women and pay for necessary care and guidance with house parents.

Amidst all the pain and sorrow in my life, there have been times of great happiness—such precious memories. Some personal accomplishments include the following: member of 4-H for thirteen years, played French horn for six years, being "Claree the Clown" for Dayton's Doll Review, and knighted by St. Paul Winter Carnival Royal Ambassadors King Boreas and Vulcanus Rex in 1991. I also have wonderful memories of seeing stunning land formations that God created: Crystal Cave in Spring Valley (Wisconsin), Redwood Forest (California), top of Pikes Peak, headwaters of the Mississippi River in Itasca State Park, the Louisiana Bayou, Mt. Denali and about half of the 800 mile oil pipeline in Alaska (view from an airplane), Grand Canyon, Mendenhall Glacier (north of Juneau), the Badlands of North Dakota (view from a helicopter), top of Banff in Alberta, Canada. City skylines have also been viewed from the top of Sears Tower (Chicago), the top of IDS building (Minneapolis), the top of Empire State building, and World Trade Center. I have seen the Hoover Dam, the Golden Gate Bridge, and the Gateway Arch, and walked across the Chapel Bridge in Lucerne, Switzerland. My travels have included visiting the Ellis Island Immigration Museum, Margaret Woodbury Strong Doll Museum in Rochester (New York), Holocaust History Museum in Jerusalem, and Alaska Native Tribal Museum in Anchorage.

Chapter 32

GOD WAS THERE ALL THE TIME

$\mathcal{L}$ooking back on my life, I can see how God was with me all the time. He took me across dry dusty plains, through heavy snowstorms while traveling over mountain passes with chains on my car; and through rugged, majestic scenery while enjoying a bag lunch with the boys on top of a mountain. He was there while I gazed at the mountain ranges on a long summer day of light. He guided us slowly through the narrows on a ferryboat at night. It seemed we could reach out and touch the high cliffs and only look up to see the sky. On winter evenings, God gave us a beautiful light show on the black canvas sky with dancing and sizzling aurora borealis (Northern Lights) in greens and blues. He gave Edna and me a large double rainbow that stretched from one side of the sky to the other while we were driving, but lost, in Oklahoma. He took Jack and me through the terrible turbulent waters of Crooked Lake in Saskatchewan to safety on the nearest shore. We were also kept safe by His guiding hands on the long trip from Saskatchewan to Milwaukee, Wisconsin—driving at times on glare ice —straight through in hopes of visiting a loved one, who was dying.

God comforted me through the quiet night watches in the hospital when I was alone and too restless to sleep. I also felt the closeness of my Savior while watching Marvin as he neared death and I could "Praise the Lord" because soon Marvin was going to be at peace in Christ.

The Lord guarded me through the experience of two earthquakes in Alaska. The Lord guided the boys and me while we traveled safely in our new VW bus through the narrow gorges along the Columbia River in Canada. And, again He protected us while on the long Canadian train ride—it seemed like we would run into the water or over the cliffs.

I love to see His cattle on a thousand hills and fields with new growth or golden harvesting and the beauty of the valleys that I can thank God for because He is there for us, too. Many days God shows me His GLORY through the windows of His clouds as sunbeams break through them and I know He is on His throne and all will be right with my part of His world. My family and I have looked up at the wonderful dark sky as the moon moved over us and thought of grandparents and relatives around the world who see the same moon. Only God can direct and illuminate the heavens to magnify His glory, His might, and His power to show us His love and faithfulness.

God never sleeps nor slumbers! If you are looking, you can see Him, too.

Chapter 33

I AM SINGLE, YET NOT ALONE!

*W*ho am I right now? Tonight?

I am single again. I am lonely! When others are with friends or spouses, I am alone. Couples and entire families are coming and going. They're hugging and kissing. Even when friends and acquaintances gather around large tables, there isn't always seating available for a single person.

It used to hurt when I saw a fellow with his arm wrapped around his wife or a couple walking close together, and especially when parents gather the family to come or go and I walk alone.

I have lonely evenings! Turmoil, rejection, depression, feelings of no hope—all of these emotions I have experienced in my life. The evening hours spent alone seem to pass slowly.

I can read through the Bible and see the many times God used single people to serve Him and share or teach many. These people are of different ages, too, and I try to relate to their lives and conditions at that time.

Most of us who are single were not put into this situation because we desired it. Maybe you've gone through a negative situation that left you single and have gathered a lot of emotional "garbage" that is too heavy to carry. Forgiveness cleans the hurt relationship again.

Perhaps there is much confusion in your home and your relationship with a loved one has become a battleground and you often lose and get hurt. Or, you might feel very much alone even though you are not living a life as a single. Most of our down times are emotional, not spiritual. They're usually feelings, not faith.

Do you feel like you have been in God's waiting room too long? In fact, I had a list of requirements for the perfect mate. My list kept getting longer and longer so I told God about it one day and asked for guidance. Days later, I wondered if God heard my prayer. After awhile, I wondered if there really was a God who loved me.

All during that time, He knew where I was. I'm so glad God tells us about singles in the Bible and how He used them.

- Naomi—a widow who lost her husband and both sons—brought Ruth back to her homeland; had a supportive role in the lineage of Jesus.
- Ruth—Moabite widow, daughter-in-law to Naomi—gleaned the fields for food; became a wife of Boaz, a wealthy man; grandmother to King David.

- David—youngest son in his family; worked as a shepherd; anointed as king.

- Esther—foster child, raised by a cousin (widower)—a Jew who became a queen! For such a time as this in God's plan!

- Joseph—whose mother being his father's favorite wife; traumatized by older brothers and sold as a slave; spent time in prison; groomed to be the second in command in Egypt; later saved his entire family and the country of Egypt from starvation.

- Mary—betrothed to Joseph; teenager who got pregnant—gave birth to Jesus.

- Timothy—young man with a godly mother's influence.

- Paul—rounded up Christians to kill them; became a follower of Jesus. He was known as the extra disciple, wrote many books of the New Testament.

Perhaps you have met wonderful Christian singles. I think of Hannah, the Apple Store computer trainer who helped me complete this book. Hannah told me how Jesus pursued her during many years of running away from God. In 2010, Rob, her coworker, led her "back" because of the joy he experienced in knowing Christ. She now lives to proclaim the supremacy of God in all things for the joy of all people in Christ.

God knew where these people were all the time, and He used them to further His kingdom. They were in the right place at the right time, waiting for what would come next in their lives, being prepared for it by God.

Compared to the living conditions of the people in the Bible, today, I have it easy and have advantages of what a woman can do living independently for 30 years. My sons are caring and willing, showing concern with phone calls. Most older, single people have radio, music, television, Internet, and even cars or bus transportation to GO. I needed Christian radio and my church family, so as I made what may be a last move, I knew it was important to live closer to my church.

Perhaps when we want to be a Christian we look to other Christians for guidance instead of unto Christ and the Bible. God can provide everything we need.

We are all unique individuals with special personalities. To appraise our appearance, we may look in a mirror and think "Not so bad! Looks okay! Okay!" Yet, when one's soul is desperately wicked, God knows it! God gave us a plan for that in John 3:16. It's called becoming "born again."

If a broken heart is all you have to give to the Lord, Jesus is a big Savior. In fact, it's about 16 inches from your head to your heart. If you believe what Jesus did for you only in your head and do not accept Him into your heart, you will miss Heaven by 16 inches!

Most of all, it's best for me to spend time in devotions, which is Bible reading, devotional messages, and to go through my prayer list every morning before activities take over the day. When I am really, really lonely, I take a nap and wake up refreshed, feeling okay again. I see others around me and remember it could be worse. I feel the presence of the Lord almost always unless I'm avoiding that closeness. I am His and He is mine even when He is yours. Let's just praise the Lord!

You may at times feel lonely but you never need to be alone! There is life for you and it's called "Victory in Jesus!" He paid the price for your sins many years ago by dying on the cross for you. The truth will set you free! God's love becomes your foundation and gives you joy and peace in your life. You can get acquainted with your Bible by starting in 1 John where God's love is explained and to learn that we are assured of eternal life through faith in Christ.

Chapter 34

MY LAST & FOREVER HOME

*H*eaven is described in the book of Revelation as well as throughout the Bible. No tears or grief, no devil and his angels, no darkness or sin, no need of lights—heaven is all righteousness, singing, and worshipping the Lord, and we will wear white robes. Believers will be joint heirs and, like Him, will live in a specially prepared place for us. We will receive crowns of Joy, Glory, Life, and/or Righteousness, rewards and treasures. Everything will be beautiful, glorious, pearl gates, gold streets, precious gems and stones. A river will run through Heaven. The Tree of Life can be seen and a wedding banquet will be held.

In the first verse of the Bible we read, "In the beginning, God…" In the last ten verses of the Bible, Jesus tells us again about His coming. How special it is for us to read the end of the BOOK and realize we are reading His last invitation to us for He is coming soon and quickly!

I actually "placed my order" for this home in Heaven on July 23, 1970, at the age of thirty-three, after talking to my pastor in my kitchen. Over the years I have come to grasp fully the enormity of what this means. The first time I went forward was at Red Rock Church Camp at Medicine Lake at the age of nine to "know" Jesus; however, no one talked to me about what this means. At least I left knowing I was still lost without a Savior, even though I didn't know what to do. Then in 1969 my sister, Winnie, and I went to a neighbor's Baptist Church to hear a great singer and his testimony. While Dale Lundgren sat in a wheelchair, he concluded his program with the song, "Like the Woman at the Well." He sang and I wept as he shared his touching testimony. I answered that call to step out and walk forward—again, but no one counseled me. So life moved on and I had a hard time forgetting that service. TODAY I have the blessed assurance that Jesus is my Savior.

Before I'm called HOME, I have a new job and experience to live out. One of my favorite women of the Bible is Esther because of her faith and courage to go before her husband, the king, with a request to save her people. She fasted, prayed, and prepared herself for the moment she must plea for her people because the king didn't know she was a Jew. A great line—FOR SUCH A TIME AS THIS—in a great story of love—God spares the lives of the Israelites again.

For the last five years, I have experienced tremors and had questions about what they could be. Doctors checked my walking and my rigidity and a few other things and came up with nothing. I have given away four small shelves that once held my small dolls and delicate little treasures. When cleaning and holding one, I would start to shake. After breaking quite a few, it seemed I needed to deal with this problem. To save my favorite little miniatures, I allowed a few more layers of dust to collect on them. Gradually I have been "de-cluttering" more areas of my apartment. Now the symptoms have really exploded in truth—Parkinson's disease.

For the first time in my life I had a new response to the nurses who greeted and inquired, "How are you today?" by answering, "I'm not feeling good at all."

Emotionally—I'm usually a 10++. I can weep with you, cry when I'm happy and feeling overjoyed, and cry when someone hurts or feels very sad, or laugh when I'm tickled.

So, following many tests, I firmly now know that I am facing a GOLIATH right in front of everything in my life. Even though there is NO cure for Parkinson's disease at this time, there are medications to help me tolerate the symptoms. I'm grateful that the research is continuing. However, the question remains: What can I squeeze into what is left of my life? Sean has asked, "What do you want to do and where do you still want to go?" My response was, "I have been to as many places as I care to visit unless it be a trip with you, Sean. That can be close or far and just to the clinic if need be."

As the disease progresses, I'm sure that it will be hard to give up the errands by car, but it will be cheaper. And, I will know when I can't be safe on the streets or highways. At that time, I will tell my sons to take the car away. I think when I have to give up the car keys, I will have to check my ego at the door and accept the fact that I wouldn't be safe on the roads.

Well, I hope to keep my sense of humor in situations—like the time I was sitting next to Donna during communion. I usually use my right hand to lift a little cup out of the tray and place it on her Bible for her to grasp. However, that time during the service, I picked up the little cup with my left hand without thinking. The tremors in my hand blew the whole routine. I dumped the liquid down the inside of my left leg and into my shoe. I checked! It wasn't on the carpet so I kept my head down, turned toward Donna, and said "Oops!" as I raised my eyebrows. We looked at each other and started to laugh and continued smiling while the deacon helped her and then me! I think the deacons had a meeting just to determine what to do with Donna and me!

During a visit with Tessie, my daughter-in-law, I blurted out the question: "What do you think I will actually die from if I don't get hit by a truck in my parking lot?"

She replied, "Oh I know that! You won't be able to turn over in bed, your vision will get worse, and you won't be able to taste food. It will become harder to eat and you'll lose weight. Before long you won't be able to breathe and then you'll die." Everybody has advice and story examples about Parkinson's for me. I'll also have plenty of people to visit with if I just tell them about Parkinson's.

My mom had also been a widow for many years. One day I asked her, "Mom, how long do you plan ahead for?" She said, "Oh, I think about five years, and then during the next year I just add another year for five again." After hearing this comment,

Doug said to me, "Mom, how about you look forward to ten years and I will remind you."

More about what I'm facing: My primary care doctor has completed all kinds of tests and solved problems to confirm it is mainly deteriorating spine—called condosium, illius, osteitis, and scoliosis of the lumbar spine. My neurologist, a doctor of hope, has been very thorough.

Oh, what a comfort it is to know that He is my personal God. I am part of the fellowship of the unashamed. I have Holy Spirit power. The die has been cast. I've stepped over the line. The decision was made: I am now a disciple of His. I will not look back, let up, slow down, back away or be still. My past is redeemed. My present makes sense. My future is secure. I am finished and done with stressed living, sight walking, small planning, colorless dreams, tamed visions, worldly talking, cheap giving, and dwarfed goals. I no longer need preeminence, prosperity, position, promotions, or popularity. I do not have to be right, first recognized, praised, regarded, or rewarded. I now live by faith, lean on His presence, and walk by His patience. I am lifted by prayer and I labor by power. My face is set. My goal is Heaven! My road is narrow and my way is rough. My guide is reliable and my mission is clear. I cannot be bought, compromised, detoured, lured away, deluded, or delayed. I will not give up, hush up, or let up. I will go on until Jesus comes and work until He stops me. I am a disciple of Jesus. I love that I can talk to God about anything—every joy, problem, pain, heartache, and all of my weakest frailties.

RECEIVING GOD'S PLAN OF SALVATION

You, too, can have peace in knowing that your sins have been forgiven and that there is a special place in Heaven prepared for you! Read the following verses aloud. Ask God to forgive your sins and claim these truths.

Romans 3:23 — For all have sinned and come short of the glory of God.

Romans 6:23 — For the wages of sin is death, but the gift of God is eternal life through Jesus Christ our Lord.

Romans 5:8 — But God commendeth his love toward us, in that, while we were yet sinners, Christ died for us.

Romans 10:9–10, 13 — That if thou shalt confess with thy mouth the Lord Jesus and shalt believe in thine heart that God hath raised Him from the dead, thou shalt be saved. For with the heart man believeth unto righteousness; and with the mouth confession is made unto salvation. For whosoever shall call upon the name of the Lord shall be saved!

If you have read this, declared to God that you are a sinner, asked Him to forgive your sins, and acknowledged that Jesus died on the cross for your sins, sign your name and the date below. Make sure to start listening and reading and talking about His WORD. Seek out a believer in Jesus for a prayer partner or spiritual mentor.

The New Name in Heaven: _____

Date Today: _____

ave you let Jesus change you? Do you stand for God's principles and guard what you think, say, and see? Do you help around your home? Speak words of blessings over family members? Choose godly friends? Correct bad habits? In Proverbs 6 we are told that doing the right thing brings honesty to people.

Today, may you touch Jesus so that others may know Him and be blessed. Right now let Him change your life.

Holy Father,

I am one of the readers, standing on the threshold of the rest of my life. I give you my heart, soul, and body. I seek higher learning and specialties, wisdom, and knowledge. I am seeking my future. Please be real to me. Show me your best—your Son in my life.

I am surrounded by greed and pleasures of materialism and new age allurements. I pray for discernment of sin and truths and to choose wisely. Allow the Holy Spirit to guide and help me stay honest, pure, kind, and generous while serving you, Lord.

In Jesus' name, I pray. Amen.

After I did ask Jesus to forgive my sins, I was eager to learn all that I could from the Bible. For me, Heaven became much more than billows of clouds where the angels lived (or sat all day). Wow! I read that the heavens declare the glory of God (Psalm 19:1) and His righteousness (Psalm 50:6 and 97:6).

There are three heavens mentioned in the Bible.

- First Heaven—space within Earth's atmosphere (Deuteronomy 10:14; Matthew 6:20, 26; Revelation 20:1)
- Second Heaven—space beyond Earth's atmosphere (Psalm 19:1, Isaiah 40:22)
- Third Heaven—the Father's paradise throne room (II Corinthians 12:2, Luke 23:43)

What a glorious day that will be when the trumpet sounds and in a twinkling of the eye we are taken up into Heaven to live with the Lord! Believers will be joint heirs and live in this specially prepared place. (Heaven is also described in Rev. 2.) I look forward to becoming a citizen of Heaven along with many loved ones and live there without pain or worries. We will worship the Lord! All is peace and truth.

FAVORITE RECIPES

Crazy Cake
(Doug's Favorite Cake—very moist!)

3 cups flour

2 cups sugar

2 tsp. soda

⅓ cup cocoa

¾ cup oil

2 tsp. vinegar

2 cups water

1 tsp. salt

Combine the ingredients in a bowl and mix well. Pour into an ungreased pan and bake at 350 degrees for 35 minutes.

Best Chocolate Bars Ever
(Jan's Recipe)

1 stick butter

1-12 oz pkg. semisweet chocolate chips

1-12 oz pkg. butterscotch chips

1 cup chunky peanut butter

1 cup miniature marshmallows

2 cups Rice Krispies® cereal

In a double boiler, melt butter, chocolate chips, and butterscotch chips. Add peanut butter and marshmallows and stir until blended. Remove from heat. Mix this with cereal in a large bowl. Press mixture into a buttered 9 x 13 inch pan. Use waxed paper or a buttered spatula to press down the mixture to level it. Refrigerate until cold and then cut into pieces.

Hot Crab & Shrimp Soufflé
(Clare & Katie's Recipe)

10–12 slices white bread (remove crusts)

Mixture for spread:

1 can crab

1 can shrimp

½ cup mayonnaise

½ medium onion, chopped

½ green pepper, chopped

Other ingredients:

3 cups milk

4 eggs

1-8 oz. can cream of mushroom soup

1 cup grated cheese

paprika

Butter half of the bread slices and place face down in 9 x 13 inch pan. In a bowl, mix together the ingredients for crab and shrimp mixture. Spread the mixture over the bread in the pan. Butter one side of the remaining bread slices. Place those buttered slices on the mixture, facing up. Beat eggs and milk together in bowl. Pour over the bread in pan. Refrigerate the dish overnight. Bake at 325 degrees for 15 minutes. Remove from oven and spread mushroom soup over the top. Sprinkle cheese and paprika on top of the soup. Bake 45–60 minutes.

Turkey Cheese Lasagna
(Doug & Tessie's Recipe)

Lasagna noodles

Filling mixture:

1-8 oz. can cream of chicken soup

1-8 oz. can cream of mushroom soup

4 cups fully cooked turkey, diced

1 cup onion, chopped

1-2 cup black olives, chopped

¼ cup pimentos, chopped

½ tsp. garlic salt

5 cups Velvetta cheese, shredded

1 cup Parmesan cheese, grated

Boil lasagna according to directions on package and drain. Place a layer of noodles on the bottom of greased 9 x 13 pan. Mix the soups together in bowl. Layer the filling mixture on the noodles and then place remaining noodles and cheese on top of mixture. Bake at 350 degrees for 40-45 minutes. Remove from heat and let the lasagna rest for 10 minutes before serving. (Very good!)

Baked Salmon
(Doug & Tessie's Recipe)

salmon, about 12 inches in length
spinach leaves

Mixture for stuffing:

⅓ cup sour cream

½ cup cream cheese

1 tbsp. lemon juice, freshly squeezed

browned bacon pieces

minced onion, garlic and dill

seasonings, as desired

Place spinach leaves in bottom of the pan. Mix together the ingredients in a bowl and stuff the salmon. Set the salmon on the spinach and then cover with more spinach leaves. Add some fresh asparagus and sausage (cut into pieces) alongside the salmon. Add a small amount of water in the pan and then cover with foil. Bake at 350 degrees for 40 minutes.

Fish Chowder

Brown cut up bacon in a medium or large kettle. Add chopped celery, minced onion, and 3–10 potatoes (peeled and chopped). Add water to cover and boil until potatoes are soft or mushy. Add salt, pepper, parsley flakes, garlic powder or minced garlic, and a good amount of cut up white fish (bones removed). Continue cooking. Keep mixture thick until fish is cooked. Add milk and 2 cups of cream and heat until hot enough to serve.

Sour Dough Blueberry Pancakes

To make sour dough starter: Use pancake mix that only needs water added! Pour 3 cups of pancake mix into a bowl. Add water as indicated on the box. Add 4–5 tbsp. bacon grease to the mixture and stir. Fill a quart jar with this mixture and refrigerate for 2 weeks.

To make pancakes, using a large bowl combine 2 cups of dry pancake mix from box, 2 cup of sour dough starter, and water as directed on package. Stir to blend ingredients. Pour some of the prepared batter back into the jar to replenish the sour dough starter and refrigerate it. Drain the blueberries and add to the batter in the bowl by folding them in gently. Fry the pancakes on a hot greased griddle until both sides are golden brown.

ACKNOWLEDGMENTS

I am grateful for my ancestors from Holland and those who came here on the *Mayflower* (William Brewster, John Alden, and William Mullins), the special parents God chose for me, and my brother and sisters, my cousins, and my family. My playmates—Kay, Kathleen and Karin—were fun and very dear to me. My wonderful and talented sons—Gregory, Douglas, and Sean—who needed me, especially when I needed a reason to live. The teachers who taught me and gave me opportunities to grow and learn the experiences needed for baby-sitting, housework, swimming, sewing, designing, canning, baking, cooking, refinishing furniture, packing and moving, and X-ray technology.

My neighbors in various locations have been wonderful and supportive. I also appreciated the efforts of medical staff members who were available for all of my family needs and crises in life. The leaders for youth and Scouts, my co-workers, and movers were special, and most of all, "Thank you, Lord" for the integrity and role modeling of these friends and relatives.

Thanks to those who taught me to do public speaking and eventually travel and speak to many groups with dolls and deliver a salvation message. Many pastors and wives have a special place in my heart for bringing me closer to the Lord—Pastor Ernie and Rachel Jones in Alaska, Pastor Jensen and Loretta in Oakdale, Pastor Will and Sharon Peterson, Pastor Bruce and Marilyn Henry in Shoreview as well as my whole church family, Pastor Jim and Katie Harrington in Wisconsin, Pastor Paul and Lois Fredrickson, and Dale Lundgren, Pillsbury staff and students.

So many dear friends and acquaintances have stood by or walked with me. Thanks to Alice and Herman, Kirby, Jan and Mary from South Dakota, Jan and Dick from New Richmond, Harry and Marlette, Barb, Shirley, Donna, Keith, Gary, Sharon, Diane, Gloria, Linda, Janine, Edna, Geri, Moni, precious Emily (who shared her story, her life, and her "grands" with me), Katy and Jim Dear, the Posts, "Red," Curt and Darla, Lil, Vern, Rochelle, Bob and Danielle, Jon and Elizabeth, Wolters, Wynn, Gardners, Sebalds, Rich and Lucy, all the Henslins and Bertholds, Monica, and Tessie.

I would also like to acknowledge Bill Sandberg (former North St. Paul Mayor); Dr. Jack and Karen Droght; Dr. and Margaret Broman and family; Ariel; Graves; Sharon Edleman; Connie and Don; Daphne; and many business people in North St. Paul, members of Minnesota Tour Managers; staff at the Minneapolis Art Institute; Colleen (the director), staff, and board members at Metro Woman's Center.

There are many who walked with me and volunteered me for special jobs that opened new doors in my life. I want to thank Mike Hanson, my lawyer, who climbed the Appalachian Mountain Range in eight months, blind! Also, I am grateful for the work done by Mike Woodside and David Welder (the "book cover guys")! May God bless you all.

The support of those who gave sacrificially of their time—especially Sue, Leah, Lucy, and Deb—to edit this book and others who encouraged me to complete the writing has been greatly appreciated. Sean and Dave will receive the first copies!

The memories and blessings to have had the opportunity to know each of you will be cherished. And, finally, thanks to the God of the universe, who knows where we are at all times, for allowing me to write this book for His glory.

CPSIA information can be obtained at www.ICGtesting.com
Printed in the USA
LVOW06s1915031115

460950LV00001B/1/P